Acclaim

The Liberating Arts is a transformative work. Opening with an acknowledgment of the sundry forces arrayed against liberal arts education today, this diverse collection of voices cultivates an expansive imagination for how the liberal arts can mend what is broken and orient us individually and collectively to what is good, true, and beautiful.

Kristin Kobes Du Mez, author, *Jesus and John Wayne*

At their best, the humanities are about discerning what kinds of lives we should be living. But humanities education is in crisis today, leaving many without resources to answer this most important question of our lives. The authors of this volume are able contenders for the noble cause of saving and improving the humanities. Read and be inspired!

Miroslav Volf, coauthor, *Life Worth Living*

In our era of massive social and technological upheaval, this book offers a robust examination of the liberal arts, and an expansive vision for teaching them. As a scientist who believes that education should shape us for lives of reflection and action, I found the essays riveting, challenging, and inspiring. I picked it up and could not put it down.

Francis Su, author, *Mathematics for Human Flourishing*

It's a mark of how confused our society has become that anyone needs to "defend" the liberal arts, and yet the task has never been more necessary. Fortunately, in this lucid and inspiring volume, a diverse group of thinkers dispel entrenched falsehoods about the irrelevance, injustice, or uselessness of the liberal arts and remind us that nothing is more fundamental to preparing citizens to live in a pluralistic society attempting to balance the values of justice, equality, and community. They demonstrate that defending the liberal arts is not an ideological or an elitist project but a human one.

Jon Baskin, editor, *Harper's Magazine*

In this series of lively, absorbing, and accessible essays, the contributors invoke and dismantle all the chief objections to the study of the liberal arts. The result is a clarion call for an education that enables human and societal flourishing. Everyone concerned about the fate of learning today must read this book.

Eric Adler, author, *The Battle of the Classics*

The Liberating Arts

The Liberating Arts

Why We Need Liberal Arts Education

Edited by **Jeffrey Bilbro,**
Jessica Hooten Wilson,
and **David Henreckson**

Plough

Published by Plough Publishing House
Walden, New York
Robertsbridge, England
Elsmore, Australia
www.plough.com

Plough produces books and a magazine to encourage people and help them put their faith into action. We believe Jesus can transform the world and that his teachings and example apply to all aspects of life. At the same time, we seek common ground with all people regardless of their creed.

Plough is the publishing house of the Bruderhof, an international Christian community. To learn more about the Bruderhof's faith, history, and daily life, see Bruderhof.com. Views expressed by Plough authors are their own and do not necessarily reflect the position of the Bruderhof.

ISBN: 978-1-63608-0-673
26 25 24 23   1 2 3 4

Cover art by Pawel Kuczynski.

A catalog record for this book is available from the British Library.
Library of Congress Cataloging-in-Publication Data

Names: Bilbro, Jeffrey, editor. | Henreckson, David P., 1985- editor. |
    Wilson, Jessica Hooten, editor.
Title: The liberating arts : why we need liberal arts education / edited by
    Jeffrey Bilbro, Jessica Hooten Wilson, and David Henreckson.
Description: Walden, NY : Plough Publishing House, 2023. | Includes
    bibliographical references. | Summary: "A new generation of teachers
    envisions a liberal arts education that is good for everyone"-- Provided
    by publisher.
Identifiers: LCCN 2023005028 | ISBN 9781636080673 (trade paperback) |
    ISBN
    9781636080772 (ebook)
Subjects: LCSH: Education, Humanistic.
Classification: LCC LC1011 .L485 2023 | DDC 370.11/2--dc23/eng/20230208
LC record available at https://lccn.loc.gov/2023005028

Printed in the United States of America

Contents

9 Aren't the Liberal Arts a Luxury?

10 Aren't the Liberal Arts Just for Smart People?

What Are the Liberating Arts?

Practical Matters

The Editors

THE BOOK YOU ARE HOLDING is the fruit of a truly collaborative process. Our aim is not merely to mount an argument for the enduring relevance of the liberal arts; it is also to model the kind of conversation and friendship that liberal arts formation makes possible. The Covid pandemic that started in 2020 and the subsequent social unrest and economic disruption liberated us from the status quo of institutional life and provoked us to rethink the purpose of the educational vision that many of us have long touted.

Liberated from complacency and from the confines of our respective disciplines and specializations, we were liberated for friendship and the possibilities of intellectual community. Given that the words "free" and "friend" come from the same root, this is only appropriate. If we shift to the Latinate word "liberal," we recognize that these arts aim to foster liberality or generosity, the dispositions that make friendship possible. The purpose of freedom is not to pursue some kind of narcissistic self-fulfillment but to cultivate friendship with others. Hence the liberal arts aim to form us to use our freedom for these proper ends rather than squander it on lesser goods.

This book is a collaborative project and follows an admittedly unusual structure. Each of the following chapters responds to one widely held perspective that we hear in today's culture, questioning the value of the liberal arts. After briefly voicing the concerns behind each question, we offer a set of three responses to it. The first and the last we call "interludes," and they briefly offer a practical example – an organization, an experience, a practice – that implicitly responds to the question at hand. These interludes don't prescribe scalable "best practices"; rather, they intend to inspire by example and prompt readers to imagine analogous possibilities in their own lives. Between these interludes is a more discursive essay that provides a formal response to the question stated in the chapter's title. The effect we're aiming at is a kind of orchestral whole, where different voices and approaches harmonize to provide a fuller vision of what a liberal arts education might look like today.

You'll discover productive disagreements in the following pages, but this is part of modeling a good-faith conversation rather than retreating into narrow ideological groups and throwing rhetorical grenades at other camps. Some essays ground their claims in Christian texts; others begin with Aristotle or other sources. You'll even discover substantively different definitions of the liberal arts themselves: a canon of great texts; a curriculum of perennial human questions; the seven classical arts of the trivium and quadrivium; a formation in virtue and wisdom rather than a training in practical skills. Different contributors draw on these various facets of the liberal arts tradition, but we can discern a beautiful harmony among these voices.

As David Henreckson describes in the second part of this introductory chapter, the origins of this book lie in some videoconference conversations that took place in the spring of 2020. That summer, as protests against racial injustice took place across the country and the economic consequences of Covid came into focus, we decided to formalize our group and make our dialogue more public. In such an apocalyptic moment, we wanted to contemplate together what was being revealed and how we might respond. The Council for Christian Colleges and Universities (CCCU) awarded us a three-year networking grant, and this enabled us to launch a website – theliberatingarts.org – and publish a series of video and audio conversations with interlocutors from many different backgrounds about the current state and future prospects of liberal arts education.

From the first, however, our group was roiled by upheaval. Jeffrey Bilbro lost his tenured faculty position the day before the CCCU awarded us this grant, and as his institution was to be the fiduciary agent, we had to scramble to find another home institution.[1] Wheaton College agreed to serve in this role, but then a year later Noah Toly, our project member at Wheaton, left to serve as the provost of Calvin University. We had to quickly find someone else at Wheaton to join our group, and Becky Eggimann graciously and capably volunteered. This story gives just a glimpse into the personal and professional transitions many have gone through since beginning this project. In 2020, all three of us editors were committed to the institutions where we worked; now, all three of us serve at different institutions. Many of the other contributors

4

have likewise shifted jobs and institutions. This is a season of political and institutional upheaval, but that only makes this conversation about the nature and value of the liberal arts more essential. This is a time to build; may we build on the right foundation and aim at the right ends.

Many of the contributors to this volume write as Christians, from within the tradition of Christian humanism that has long been part of the liberal arts story. It goes without saying that the liberal arts are equally for those with other faiths, or none. But in editing this collection we concluded that it is appropriate for practitioners to speak from their own particular religious and philosophical traditions, not from a standpoint of artificial neutrality. Readers are encouraged to apply the insights they find useful to their own contexts and traditions.

We are grateful to all those who have contributed along the way, particularly those who agreed to record interviews with us and think in public during these fraught months. Anne Snyder and Breaking Ground, another project launched during the pandemic to think carefully about the implications of this season, supported us from the first and were delightful to partner with as we launched our website. We're particularly grateful to two students who played key roles in our endeavor: Seth Gorveatte brilliantly edited our amateur video recordings, and Sarah Soltis copyedited this book manuscript and double-checked citations.

Due to the support of the CCCU and Plough Publishing House, we are able to donate the proceeds from this book to four organizations that are doing inspiring and important work: the Catherine Project, the Clemente Course in the Humanities, Nyansa Classical Community, and the Odyssey Project. May creative and courageous institutions such as these continue to thrive, and may this book inspire others to go and do likewise.

Amid the Ruins

David Henreckson

W HEN I WAS YOUNG my family attended the church of a small congregation of Scottish Covenanters. Historically, the Covenanters were a zealous people, not shy about fighting theological battles with non-theological weapons. Their militancy mellowed out in modern times, although their doctrinal ferocity remained. Covenanters love the psalms of the Hebrew Bible – so much so, they sing them exclusively and with no musical accompaniment. In my memory, the a cappella singing in our own church may have sounded spare and raw and unforgiving, yet I came to love it: four-part harmonies plus the unpredictable fifth part contributed by the tone-deaf elder with the five daughters in calico dresses.

During these years, my family also picked up the habit of practicing Sabbath. Sundays among the Covenanters had an austere and rigorous beauty. No commerce, no dining out, and ideally no recreational sports.

I didn't do Sabbath particularly well. The coerced time of self-reflection was often uncomfortable. There was nothing else to do but, well, *contemplate* – which the ancients alleged was the pinnacle of human activity, and which I would have spurned for a mundane outing to the suburban mall.

My Sabbath practice predictably withered away during adulthood. But when a global pandemic struck and sent us all into isolation, I had occasion to read the Jewish theologian Abraham Joshua Heschel's 1951 book, *The Sabbath*. Heschel's meditations are famously and cryptically metaphysical, but his book also contains prisms of insight that stuck with me in quarantine. One particular line resonated: "Sabbath is not an occasion for diversion or frivolity; not a day to shoot fireworks or to turn somersaults, but an opportunity to mend our tattered lives; to collect rather than to dissipate time."[2]

This seems a healthy way to think about the Sabbath, somewhat more humane and certainly more intentional than the way I tried to practice it in my youth. But what would it actually mean to mend tattered lives, to collect rather than dissipate time? What *use* would that be?

The Moment of Crisis

A few weeks after my university sent me to finish the semester online in March of 2020, with the threat of furlough and possible unemployment looming on the horizon, I wrote to a group of academic friends – many of whom are contributors to this volume in one way or another. With Heschel in the back of my mind, I referred to the quarantine as a "time of enforced Sabbath."

How might we convert this period of isolation into an opportunity to reflect on our respective vocations in the troubled world of higher education?

For years those of us working in educational institutions, particularly ones with liberal arts missions, have felt the cultural and political fractures that threaten these institutions. Even so, I did not fully grasp in that moment just how unsteady these institutions were, and how under fire the practices of liberal learning they serve. Few of us did. The pandemic brought this reality into stark relief.

Within a matter of weeks, some members of the group had lost their tenured or tenure-track jobs. I was furloughed. Others, given occasion to reflect on the unstable state of higher education, voluntarily left their traditional academic positions.

These sorts of vocational crises are challenging enough in normal times. In isolation, they can feel debilitating. What this gathering of friends provided was a community in which to express frustration, dread, and occasionally hope for the future. An enforced Sabbath may not be an occasion for diversion or frivolity, but it was certainly an opportunity for communal self-reflection. The moment of crisis in early 2020 forced many of us to rethink what matters most – both personally and professionally. The pandemic sent many of us home for months. Emerging social protest movements focused our attention on systemic injustices and political divisions that threaten the order of things. Drastic economic shifts called into question the monetary value of a college degree and heightened pre-existing inequalities. Many colleges and universities "discontinued" (what a euphemism) entire departments and in some cases shuttered the entire institution.

All my friends in that initial group, and the others who have joined us along the way, have asked ourselves at one point or another: Amid the ruins, is teaching and practicing the liberal arts worth doing in such a time as this?

Facing the Challenges

In my decade of teaching, I've noticed a steadily increasing level of anxiety among my students about the purpose of their college education. A college degree no longer ensures a good job and a stable middle-class existence. Student debt has climbed so high so fast that we now commonly call it a national crisis. The pressure to perform, to succeed, to excel is more intense than ever, even as the markers for success are harder to measure and harder to attain.

Not long ago, one of my best students came to my office after class and asked me a question that has stuck with me. She said that as she was nearing graduation, after two surreal years of virtual education, everyone was asking her what she was going to *do* after college. What they were asking her, in fact, was whether she had a job lined up yet – whether her professional and financial prospects were bright. This student is exceptionally smart, and I knew she had several excellent opportunities in front of her. But she confessed that her anxiety was less about the question, "What am I supposed to *do* after college?" and more about the question: "*Who* am I supposed to *be*?"

I remember thinking, *if only more faculty and administrators were asking the same question.*

Many recent studies have looked at the complications of post-college life: five years after college, approximately three-quarters of college graduates are working in a field different from their undergraduate major.[3] And yet how many strategic plans assembled by higher education consultants take account of this variability and contingency? How many of us, including faculty in traditional liberal arts fields, equip our students with the intellectual, moral, and even spiritual virtues to weather such unpredictable futures?

When my student told me she was concerned about *who* she was supposed to *be*, she shifted the focus from career to character, and from marketability (a fuzzy concept itself) to vocation. It strikes me now that this shift in focus is precisely what is needed when the world of higher education is itself in something of a state of emergency, as so many colleges and universities (particularly small liberal arts institutions) are wondering not just how to thrive but, increasingly, how to survive declining enrollment, political conflicts, and financial uncertainty.

Yet the silver lining in all this is that in anxious times we are driven back to first principles: What really matters? What sort of person should I be, in order to do justice to my neighbor? What sorts of love should I cultivate, even when everything seems unstable? What am I called to do, personally and professionally, when things beyond my control have placed a giant question mark on the structures we once took for granted?

This is where I suspect that institutions devoted to the liberal arts, and particularly those with Christian commitments, have a unique vocation or even charism, to borrow a theological term. We have a deep moral vocabulary to draw on for moments like the present. We have a tradition of inquiry, oriented toward the pursuit of truth and beauty and goodness. We have centuries of wisdom to draw on, with voices from Confucius, Plato, and Aquinas to Mary Wollstonecraft, Frederick Douglass, Gustavo Gutiérrez, Marilynne Robinson, and Nicholas Wolterstorff.

If this is to be a time of Sabbath, we should make good use of it to mend what has long been tattered.

Visions for Hope

And yet it is hard to pursue such fundamental questions in a time of crisis and instability. With livelihoods and institutional survival at stake, it seems a luxury to talk about a liberal arts education, or the old trifecta of truth, beauty, and goodness. In these days of austerity, is there still a central place for intellectual and moral formation in the university?

These are questions that the liberal arts are supposed to help us answer. And yet, ironically, it is liberal arts education that seems most imperiled in the wake of pandemic and protest and scarcity. Under duress, it is natural to lead pragmatic lives determined by economic needs or personal preferences. It is no surprise that, in these conditions, many of us struggle to find ultimate meaning in our lives and vocations.

What kind of moral or spiritual awakening do we need in these anxious times?

In one of my favorite books on higher education, *Exiles from Eden*, Mark Schwehn writes that "academies at their best can and should become communities where the pleasures of friendship and the rigors of work are united."[4] Of course, in the midst of the pandemic, both these pleasures were quite remote. Or so it seemed at first.

The gathering of friends that constitutes this project, which we eventually named "The Liberating Arts," sustained hope for many of us when it seemed like our own academic institutions were falling apart. And in truth, this sort of community, where the pleasures of friendship and the rigors of work were united, is both the grounds for renewal of our scholarly labors and their culmination. The liberal arts themselves are not mere skills or techniques to be mastered and passed along to the young adults we happen to teach. Rather, they are a way of life, the crafts or practices by which we live out the freedom that makes us flourish as human beings. This way of life ought to cultivate in us a spirit of liberality and a communal desire to mend a tattered world, to seek justice for our neighbor, and to heal social divisions. In short, the liberal arts must liberate or they are mere semblances of wisdom masquerading as the real thing. And this liberation is most likely to happen in the company of good friends.

And so, this book is the result of many intersecting friendships, often formed amid shared anxiety and loss and shaped by sustained debate as much as by agreement. You, the reader, will encounter multiple visions for the future of liberal arts education in what follows. There will be much agreement about fundamentals, but also divergence about how to achieve the goods promised by the practice of the liberal arts. What counts as the liberal arts? What vision of human flourishing should shape our pedagogy? What are the demands of justice – with respect to gender, race, sexuality, and economic privilege – that ought to inform our educational institutions? Is the tradition hopelessly elitist? Is it too conservative? Too "woke" and progressive? How can we ensure that the errors of the past do not shape the future of the liberal arts tradition? Do we need new institutions to carry this tradition forward or can the institutions of yesterday revive and sustain this vision of educational formation? These are among the questions addressed in the following chapters.

Yet these remain live questions, and this book cannot promise a unified answer, much less one that will satisfy everyone. Nevertheless, we hope that this book offers its readers an opportunity to listen in on an ongoing public conversation. We hope this is an occasion for individuals who care deeply about intellectual and spiritual formation to pause and reflect on our calling and character in an anxious age.

Amid all the uncertainties and emergency measures and predictions of the liberal arts' demise, this book invites you to stand still and contemplate for just a few moments: What makes for a life worth living? What do we owe to each other and to the young adults who are about to venture into an unpredictable future? How might we encourage one another to mend our tattered lives, and collect the time that has been given to us?

Aren't the Liberal Arts a Waste of Time?

Who has time to spend reading old books and conversing about abstract ideas such as truth, the good life, or justice? We face many pressing issues, and nattering on about big ideas won't help us solve them. During times of crisis we need pragmatic solutions. I'm looking for actionable plans, not faculty-lounge philosophizing.

Practicing the Liberal Arts in Prison

Sean Sword

WHO HAS TIME FOR CONVERSING about old books and abstract ideas such as truth, the good life, or justice?

One clear answer to this question would be: individuals confined in prison seeking a path toward rehabilitation, as well as corrections officials who want to protect the public while simultaneously providing prisoners an opportunity for growth.

The confines of prison compel individuals who seek a path of rehabilitation to engage in a soul-searching process and reflect on various aspects of a life gone astray. Most of that reflection is done in isolation, where human qualities such as kindness, civility, and love are absent. Because we are relational beings, those missing qualities severely restrict a proper reception of any type of education. When the Michigan Department of Corrections allowed the opportunity for prisoners to participate in a faith-based education, the liberal arts were liberated – freed from their confinement to schools to break through prison walls.

This liberal arts program has created a space for kindness, civility, and love to flourish at the Richard A. Handlon campus in Ionia, Michigan. Students and staff have become better-integrated human beings as a result, and although rehabilitation does not happen in an instant, the liberal arts play a key role in the prisoner's restoration to society.

Through the generosity of donors who wish to participate in the restorative process, Calvin University and Calvin Theological Seminary provided me with education in the liberal arts while I was in prison. This experience enhanced my ability to apply discussions of truth, the good life, and justice to my life in two ways. First, it provided me with a path to redemption and reconciliation through the teachings of Christ, which gave balance and clarity in a spiritual sense. Second, I was attracted to the idea of servant leadership, geared toward restoration of my relationship with society starting with staff and prisoners within the facility. Together, these two aspects served as a much-needed balm for the shame of past wrongs and a solid foundation for life as a returning citizen in society.

Guiding me toward a vocation and a vision of God's kingdom, the faith-based component of my education has been instrumental, since it is most responsible for my relationship with professors, staff, and other students. These relationships are about more than just the exchange of information; they are about inquiry into truth, the good life, justice, and love in relation to others – reflecting the character of Christ and the relational qualities most yearned for in the prison setting.

This educational ministry carries over into the overwhelming expression of support that I have received since being released from prison and continuing my studies on Calvin's main campus at Knollcrest. Students and faculty have welcomed me with open arms. I attend classes and campus events brimming with confidence that I have a home within this community. My trust in humanity has been restored, and the process of reconciliation with God and his creation is my top priority.

Another major influence in restoring my trust in humanity has been the liberal arts curriculum and the vibrant learning environment it produces at the university. It is a mirror image of what was happening at the Handlon campus where I started my courses and embarked on a serious effort at being able to trust again. Communication between prisoners, officers, and administration improved dramatically. Calvin Prison Initiative students began to engage the larger prison population as peer-to-peer mentors, tutors for the various vocational trade programs, and effective mediators who prevented violence within the facility.

At the Knollcrest campus, the liberal arts forum allows students and faculty to become better educated about the criminal justice system and the lives of those within its grasp. I don't know of many educational opportunities where a twenty-year-old college student who wants to be a lawyer has a classmate who served twenty-seven years in prison. Imagine the rich content that is found in a sociology class focused on corrections and incarceration, or a statistics and probability course that studies the mean, median, and mode of incarceration numbers at all levels of government. That is what the liberal arts provides: an opportunity to learn from each other based on life experiences, academic instruction, and direction toward vocation in society.

The prisoners and staff who make up the population of a prison are a microcosm of what is found in the larger societies we live in. I was sentenced to life without parole at the age of seventeen for crimes against society. The liberal arts have exposed me to topics such as truth, the good life, and justice and allowed me to restore my relationship with God and his creation in a way that has changed my life forever.

What Is Time For?

Zena Hitz

I N HIS *CONFESSIONS*, Saint Augustine describes a
fascinating moment in his conversion to the Christian
faith. At the time, he was a successful teacher of
rhetoric in Milan, living with his longtime concubine and
their son. He had a group of close friends and was breaking
away from the Manichaeans, the gnostic cult he had spent
many years with, studying and teaching. Overwhelmed by
the limits of human knowledge, he was increasingly skep-
tical that anyone could come to know the truth about how
to live. He oscillated back and forth between skepticism
that anything certain could be known and his budding
interest in the Christian faith, the latter nurtured by
hearing the preaching of Ambrose, bishop of Milan. He
described his internal dialogue at the time:

> But where can truth be sought? *When* can it be sought?
> Ambrose has no time. There is no time for reading. Where
> should we look for the books that we need? Where and
> when can we obtain them? From whom can we borrow

them? Fixed times must be kept free, hours appointed, for the health of the soul. Great hope has been aroused.... Why do we hesitate to knock at the door which opens the way to all the rest? Our pupils occupy the mornings; what should we do with the remaining hours? Why do we not investigate our problem? But then when should we go to pay respects to our more influential friends, whose patronage we need? When are we to prepare what our students are paying for? When are we to refresh ourselves by allowing the mind to relax from the tension of anxieties?[1]

Augustine's language can be lofty and remote. But here is one of his great human moments. He wants to know how to live. He is not worried about discovering a truth that might spoil his career or require him to leave his concubine. Really! He doesn't have time, that's all – he's *too busy*, between his students and his patrons, oh, and Ambrose is too busy too. Everyone's too busy. He doesn't have time to read. Besides, he doesn't have time to get the books. Too bad for Augustine – he can't figure out the best way to live. He's too busy.

Earlier in the same section of the *Confessions*, Augustine describes how busy Ambrose is. Ambrose *is* busy. Bishops of that time were expected to adjudicate disputes between members of their flock, an endless and demanding task. The life of a bishop was so hectic, in fact, that later in life, after he had become Catholic, Augustine would do almost anything to avoid being appointed one. The historian Peter Brown describes him as going from town to town in Africa, carefully avoiding any occasion in which he might be appointed bishop by acclamation. Alas, he was tricked: in Hippo he found himself at a liturgy that became his election as bishop. Tears poured down his face as he realized his life of philosophical leisure was over.

Yet Augustine describes with reverence what Ambrose does in the brief moments in which he does not have an appointment. He reads silently. He does not steal away to a quiet place. Ambrose just sits and reads in the midst of his busyness, passing his eyes over the page.

> I could not put the questions I wanted to put to him as I wished to do. I was excluded from his ear and from his mouth by crowds of men with arbitrations to submit to him, to whose frailties he ministered. When he was not with them, which was a very brief period of time, he restored either his body with necessary food or his mind by reading. When he was reading, his eyes ran over the page and his heart perceived the sense, but his voice and tongue were silent. He did not restrict access to anyone coming in, nor was it customary even for a visitor to be announced. Very often when we were there, we saw him silently reading and never otherwise. After sitting for a long time in silence (for who would dare to burden him in such intent concentration?) we used to go away. We supposed that in the brief time he could find for his mind's refreshment, free from the hubbub of other people's troubles, he would not want to be invited to consider another problem.[2]

Ambrose has chosen to use his spare snatches of time to return within himself, to become an island of stillness. His reading, certainly, is an example of *leisure*.

WHAT IS LEISURE, and why is it necessary for human beings? The leisure that I am interested in is not the first thing you may imagine: bingeing Netflix on the couch, lounging at the beach, attending a festive party with friends, or launching yourself from the largest human catapult for the thrill of it. The leisure that is necessary for human beings is not just a break from real life, a place where we rest and restore ourselves in order to go back to work. What we are after is a state that looks like the culmination of a life.

Let's pause and ask ourselves: What parts of our lives seem to be the culminating parts, the days or hours or minutes where we are living life to the fullest? When do you stop counting the time and become fully present to what you are doing? What sorts of activities are you engaged in when this takes place?

We do many things instrumentally, for the sake of something else: eat breakfast to calm hunger pains, exercise to stay healthy, work for money. Other things we do for pleasure: play cards, go for hikes, read, or build model airplanes. Some things evidently both are instrumental and bring us delight: we work for money, but sometimes also for the love of our work; we fish to eat, but also for the sport of it.

We have many goals, but certain goals have an ordering effect on others. We either choose our career to permit leisure time with our family, or we choose to minimize familial obligations to allow free upward growth in our career. Our ultimate end, family in the first case, success in the second, frames and structures our other pursuits. We trade a freer schedule for more money or sacrifice a higher salary for more time to pursue our heart's desire. The structuring effect of some goals over others suggests that we have a *basic orientation*, determined by our ultimate end, the goal that structures all our other choices. Such a goal is our highest good, whether we have chosen it as such, or whether it has grown haphazardly out of inward or social pressures. That highest good or ultimate end might be wealth, status, family life, community service, enjoyment of the natural world, knowledge of God, writing novels, or even the pursuit of mathematical truth.

We may not know what in the soup of our desires matters most to us. Often we discover it in times of trial or crisis: a difficult choice at work, a family member in a hospital bed – in other words, when we face sickness, poverty, or moral compromise.

What would happen if we tried to organize our lives around merely instrumental pursuits? We are not likely to order our lives around grocery shopping or paying taxes. But what about earning money? If I pack my swim bag, put on shoes, get my keys, and drive my car to the pool, only to find it closed, my goal of swimming is frustrated, and my string of actions is in vain. Suppose the pool is open and I get to swim: Why do I do it? I swim for the sake of health. I want to be healthy so I can work. I work for the sake of money. And the money is for the sake of the food, drink, housing, recreation, and exercise – all of which make it possible for me to work.

I have described a life of utter futility. If I work for the sake of money, spending money on basic necessities, and if my life is organized around working, my life is a pointless spiral of work for the sake of work. It is like buying ice cream, immediately selling it for cash, and then spending the proceeds on ice cream (which one sells once again, and so on). It is just as tragic as working for money and getting crushed by a falling anvil on the way to cash the paycheck. For this reason Aristotle argued that there must be some activity or activities beyond work – leisure, for the sake of which we work and without which our work is in vain. Leisure is not merely recreation, which we might undertake for the sake of work – to relax or rest before beginning to labor anew. It is an activity or set of activities that could count as the culmination of all our endeavors. For Aristotle, only contemplation could be ultimately satisfying in this way: the activity of seeing and understanding and savoring the world as it is.

WHAT DOES CONTEMPLATIVE LEISURE look like in real life? I've collected a few examples. Renée, heroine of the French art-house film *The Hedgehog*, is the concierge of a wealthy apartment building in Paris. Her work is humble – cleaning, taking mail, organizing the workmen. But her real life is elsewhere – in a hidden room behind her kitchen, where she reads philosophy, literature, and the classics.

Renée echoes a similar figure in an earlier film, *Ali: Fear Eats the Soul*, by the German director Rainer Werner Fassbinder. Emmi is a middle-aged cleaning lady, at the bottom of the social barrel. To the horror of her xenophobic children and neighbors, she falls in love with a younger Moroccan guest worker. They make a strange couple, crossing age groups and races. But they find a refuge that two people sometimes find, a space away from demeaning judgments, where they contemplate in one another their simple, vulnerable humanity. In one scene, they sit alone at an outdoor café, surrounded by fallen autumn leaves, holding hands and gazing into each other's eyes. This film is more tragic than *The Hedgehog*, since the protagonists rely on each other for their refuge, and since they carry within themselves the expectations from their social world – expectations which destroy their relationship.

The leisured contemplation in loving relationships is worth mentioning, since it is the type most commonly recognized and valued today. But there is also the more traditional, intellectual form of leisure: Renée sequestered in her room reading, cat curled at her feet. Consider the medieval and renaissance paintings of Mary at the Annunciation. These images, drawing on early Christian writers, often picture Mary reading a book. Here is Ambrose:

> She, when the angel entered, was found at home in privacy, without a companion, that no one might interrupt her attention or disturb her; and she did not desire any women as companions, who had the companionship of good thoughts. Moreover, she seemed to herself to be less alone when she was alone. For how should she be alone, who had with her so many books, so many archangels, so many prophets?[3]

Images of study and intellectual life as a leisured refuge are older than Christianity: Plato describes his teacher Socrates as lost in thought, standing all dressed up on the threshold of a dinner party, having forgotten where he is.

The great mathematician Archimedes was by legend so lost in his theorems that he did not notice the Romans invading his city and was killed by a Roman soldier when he insisted on finishing his proof before going to the Roman officials. Later writers gave him last words: "Don't disturb my circles."

Nor are these images only in fiction or legend or ancient tradition. Albert Einstein was a failure as a graduate student in physics and could not get an academic job. He found work as a patent clerk; it was in the patent office, in his spare time, that he wrote the extraordinary papers on the photoelectric effect and Brownian movement that changed the face of the mathematical study of nature. He called the patent office "my worldly cloister where I hatched all my most beautiful ideas."

Prisoners have been among the most splendid exemplars of leisure. The Russian dissident Irina Ratushinskaya describes prisoners in transport passing poetry to one another, written on scraps of paper. Ratushinskaya herself, during her own imprisonment in Siberia, scratched poems onto soap bars with matchsticks. Once she had memorized them, she washed them away. Later she wrote them out on cigarette paper to be smuggled to the West.[4] Irina Dumitrescu writes of a Romanian officer imprisoned in Siberia who wrote out poems he had memorized in school with ink that he made out of blackberries. Other Romanian prisoners tapped poetry in Morse code through the walls of the prison, or taught each other languages in silence, with letters coded by knots on a piece of string.

What explains the power of these examples? I think it is because they show the dignity of human beings, the fact that a human being is not reducible to his or her social uses. The forcible diminishment of the prisoners is an attempt at thought control, to make them think or speak as authorities would like them to. Likewise, the commonplace diminishment of working people such as building supervisors or cleaning ladies does not suppress the splendor of a human being, or it does so only superficially. Mary, after all, is an unwed teenage mother. Her prayerful and studious solitude suggests a dignity beyond the social uses set for young women of her era: sexual pleasure, the extension of clans and bloodlines. We see all these people choosing forms of leisure – thinking, study, prayer, love – in the face of opposition, resistance, or outright hostility.

These are, however, exceptional human beings. Sometimes, hostile circumstances make leisure very difficult or even impossible. Jack London tells the semi-autobiographical tale of Martin Eden in his novel by that name. Martin is working class but is giving himself an intensive education through reading and study. However, he has to eat, and at some point he takes the only job he can find, working in a laundry for fifteen-hour days, six days a week. This type of work is so exhausting that after only a week, he is unable to read. After several weeks, he is unable to think and takes refuge in cheap pleasures.

Likewise, consider the situation of the Amazon warehouse worker, as described by journalist James Bloodworth.[5] Thanks to the choices of their company executives, the workers are hired by a temp company, which monitors their every move with surveillance bracelets, penalizes them for bathroom breaks or illness, holds out the promise of rewards that never materialize, changes schedules capriciously, docks their pay, sometimes by mistake, and in general makes workers so riven with anxiety and exhausted by overwork that cheap pleasures become enormously attractive, even to those to whom they had not been previously. So the capacity for leisure can be made more difficult, or even impossible, by circumstances.

Now, however, we face a puzzle. If leisure is what our lives aim at, how could we fail to achieve it – we, that is, who are not deprived by circumstances? What are the obstacles in us to attaining our highest good? How is it that we ourselves, through our own choices, diminish our dignity?

The example of restless, workaholic Augustine is important. It is not true that he doesn't have time. The fact is he, like us, is of two minds about leisure. He wants it and he doesn't want it. He's committed to other things: his job, his students, his patrons, his rest, and his social advancement above all. That is worth dwelling on for a moment. But there is a deeper problem: It's not just that he doesn't want to make sacrifices; he is actively avoiding leisure. He, like us, is afraid of it.

Work in itself, of course, can be a good thing. It is the way that we serve our communities. That is true if we work at a business that supplies something that people need to live; or if we work to raise our children; or if we work as teachers, doctors, lawyers, electricians, garbage collectors, health care aides, and so on.

Yet good things, as we know from everyday experience, are not always good. Food is a good thing, until we overeat. Sex is a good thing, but we can use it in demeaning or dehumanizing or otherwise harmful ways. I think it may already be clear how we misuse work. After all, how many of us really think of it as service, rather than as a vehicle for money or status? How many of us are genuinely open to serving our communities however we are most needed, even if serving that need doesn't pay much or has a low social status – if, for instance, it will be scorned by people we talk to on airplanes?

Nowhere are our true feelings about work clearer than in the growth of jobs which pay well and offer high status, but which have little to no social value. Sociologist David Graeber calls them bullshit jobs.[6] (It is difficult to find a non-profane word that combines the pointlessness of these jobs with the necessary deception they involve.) Bullshit jobs are both pointless and require pretending that they are not pointless. One example: being a subcontractor to a subcontractor to the military, whose job it is to drive long distances to move furniture from one room to another. More poignant is the story of the man hired to patch a problem that the higher authorities in the company do not want fixed. He is literally paid – and paid well – to do nothing. He starts out reading novels, then starts drinking at work and taking phony work trips, trying to get himself fired. Finally, he tries to resign and gets offered a raise. His job is a necessary pretense for his superiors – they cannot let him go. What is fascinating about the stories Graeber collects is how deeply unhappy these workers are, people who have money and status without having to work for it. It seems that their hearts long for real work, for service, for connection with their communities.

We think of American culture – a culture shared with much of Western Europe – as a culture that values work. But it is not in fact *work* that we value. What we value is money and status, no matter the cost in other human goods. It is its connection with money and with status that allows work to become addictive or compulsive. After all, remember Augustine, who finds himself plenty busy, always with an end of social advancement. But let's also remember Ambrose. He has more work than anybody, but he knows how to use his breaks. His leisure shows us what he cares about most; it shows both why his work matters and why it doesn't matter.

We are not only distracted from leisure by conflicting desires for social advancement. We also fear it and resist it from inside. Our resistance to it is both powerful and devious. We can see this in the deterioration of professions or vocations strictly dedicated to leisure. For example, one could join a monastery and live obsessed with high liturgical achievements such as the perfect performance of the best music. Or one could try to work one's way up whatever social hierarchy may exist there – to be choir director, cellarer, abbot. Or one could try to be a monk or nun for the world, dedicating one's time to winning new vocations or publicity for religious life. None of these objectives is bad in itself, but their pursuit can eat away at one's humanity. A person can live in a monastery, under vows of poverty, chastity, and obedience, and still nurture the heart of a politician or social climber.

Likewise, any professor can tell you that despite ancient tradition, true leisure in academia is hard to come by. At the bottom end, hapless adjuncts manage large classes in which often virtually no learning takes place. Their grading burden is such that time for real thinking is rare. At the top end, we find a ruthless pursuit of arcane forms of status. The rush for prestige, for articles or books that make an impression, for networking, for climbing up the institutional ladder, makes much of academic life no more leisurely than the average Fortune 500 company.

Other examples of leisurely activity are no less fragile than monastic life or academic life. A life outdoors can be overtaken by advocacy or forms of competition; family life can be rotted through with a frenetic, soul-destroying race for achievement.

Leisure requires cultivation – cultivation of habits and of communities that help to form habits. The pursuit of leisure requires this effort because we resist it. Augustine does not only desire social advancement – he is also afraid of leisure itself. What is Augustine afraid of? What is it *in us* that flees from leisure? It is, simply speaking, our own emptiness. Saint John of the Cross describes the human soul as made up of great caverns, caverns constituted by our senses and their emptiness constituted by their necessary passivity, receptivity, susceptibility. We seek out distractions in order to hide from this terrifying emptiness that can only be filled with God. The emptiness is our dependence on what comes from the outside, our need to wait for God to act. This dependence and this need are objectively terrifying. What will come? An earthquake? Cancer? Joblessness? More to the point: What will we find in ourselves? That we love status and money more than we thought we did? That we don't know ourselves, or God, or what matters in our lives? Leisure turns out to be an *interior discipline*. It is not enough to simply choose a central life activity that is intrinsically leisurely. One must recognize the good of leisure and seek it out. Moreover, leisure might require *sacrifice*. A less lucrative job might permit more time with one's family. A less prestigious academic post might permit a greater focus on studying and contemplative teaching. The examples of Ambrose, Renée, and Ratushinskaya show, I hope, that leisure is worth the cost, and that it is possible.

On the Road with Marilynne Robinson

David Henreckson

THE FORMATION OF FRIENDSHIP has interested me for some time. How two (or more) individuals find themselves drawn together into a relationship of affinity touches on the *matter* and the *object* of friendship – the *what* and the *why* of friendship.

Many friendships come into being initially because of some shared pursuit or hobby or – to use Aristotle's terminology – some practical utility that may or may not last a great length of time. True friendships endure and deepen across time and circumstance for the sake of the relationship itself, not for any usefulness it may bring to the individuals involved.

In my experience, the classroom is not the best context for the creation of real friendships. There is, of course, the obvious power differential that exists between teacher and student, which ought to create appropriate boundaries that prevent intimate friendships. But even among students there is a utilitarian character to the interactions that can promote very good, practical relationships (study groups, camaraderie) but not friendship.

I have, however, seen the spark of real friendship kindled in spaces just outside the classroom, in ways that took me by surprise.

In my first teaching job, at Dordt University, the faculty body was relatively small, and most everyone knew each other, attended the same cluster of Dutch Reformed churches, and lived in the same neighborhood. We shared meals and drinks at the local coffeehouse, where grievances and rumors and anxieties about the future of higher education were shared – perhaps too liberally.

Several of us in the theology and English departments quickly discovered our common love for the novels of Marilynne Robinson (we were less unified in our estimation of her essays). It was a delight to share our thoughts on Jack Boughton, the prodigal son with a tender but wounded spirit. The letters of the aging pastor John Ames to his young son drew out strong emotions from those of us who were relatively new to fatherhood. Some of us had reservations about the ways in which Robinson addressed the problem of race in America. We agreed and argued interchangeably, but always enjoyably.

Augustine once wrote, "My weight is my love. Wherever I am carried, my love is carrying me."[7] This is a complicated idea, insofar as our loves are often disordered, limited, and misdirected: "the better the objects of [the people's] united love, the better the people, and the worse the objects of its love, the worse the people."[8] But Augustine's insight does reveal a truth, however troubling: the objects of our love in a very real sense reveal who we are.

Properly ordered loves, like friendship itself, beg for more company. When you love something well, it makes sense to want to share it.

Our shared love of Robinson's novels (four of them had been published at the time: *Housekeeping*, *Gilead*, *Home*, and *Lila*) constituted, in part, the *matter* of the friendship that existed among our small group of faculty colleagues. We wanted to share this love more broadly.

One year, I discovered that Marilynne Robinson would be headlining a conference at Wheaton College – eight hours east – near the end of the spring semester. So we plotted an extracurricular project: a joint faculty-student Marilynne Robinson book club. Each faculty member volunteered to host a discussion of one book in his or her home, providing food and drink, and each of us agreed to recruit students from across the college to participate. In my memory, none of the students had read Robinson before, but about a dozen signed up to attend – primarily because they were intrigued by the idea of joining an intellectual community with their professors in which they would be equal participants. For each session, a faculty member would meet ahead of time with one student who had agreed to facilitate conversation. Then, once the actual book club began, it was a freewheeling conversation in which anything could be brought to the table. It was the highlight of my year.

At the end of spring semester, we borrowed one of the university vans and trekked out to suburban Chicago. On the first evening of the conference, we arrived at the auditorium and sat in the front row – the students a bit awestruck by seeing Robinson herself so close.

The conference itself was wonderful, but the conversations between sessions and in the van were the real delight of the trip. Listening to the students reflect on the talks, but also on life and vocation and the other things that a liberal arts education is supposed to foster, was one of the most rewarding teaching experiences I've had.

But it was more than that. Marilynne Robinson's literary work was what brought us together. But *why* did this little extracurricular experiment work so well?

I remember the occasions when, as an undergraduate student myself, I was invited to my professors' homes, ate at their tables, played with their children, and saw their humanity and imperfections up close. I remember conversations we had about faith and science or moments when I courageously (or rashly) shared my frustration with the way the administration was handling some issue or another. It would be silly to think that the power differential between me and my professors evaporated the moment we moved from the classroom to the living room. And yet there was something about it that made for a more real companionship (even if it could not quite amount to friendship).

More than that, I like to think that the freewheeling book discussions, in which my faculty colleagues and I often *disagreed* about aspects of the novels, invited the students into a space where they saw how friends could share common objects of love and argue about them simultaneously. Robinson provided the *what* of our friendship;

the conversation and arguments and shared delight over a particular turn of phrase provided the *why*.

Few literary characters have moved me as much as Robinson's Jack Boughton, the alcoholic son of a devout but hardheaded Presbyterian minister. Jack is a man riven by competing desires and unregulated passions, bearing the scars of his father's overbearing concern masquerading as love.

In one pivotal exchange with his sister Grace, Jack confesses that despite his wanderings he has never outrun a "certain spiritual hunger." He has been well catechized by his father. He knows "the great truths" of Christian doctrine and can recite chapter and verse with ease. But still, he says, "It is possible to know the great truths without feeling the truth of them. That's where the problem lies. In my case."[9]

If students are not merely intellectual vessels to be loaded with content but lovers drawn with the force of gravity toward their shared loves, we need to create communal contexts that account for their whole humanity – mind, body, and soul. The liberal arts must be more than a determinate canon; they must be a way of life. The classroom can achieve many things, but sometimes a mussed-up living room or a road trip in a rusty Econoline van can be spaces where the *what* and the *why* of real friendship and intellectual growth flourish.

3

Aren't the Liberal Arts Elitist?

The liberal arts have always been an
exclusionary tradition that has left out
many people: those without money, those
without high IQ, people with disabilities,
women, and racial minorities.

The Odyssey Project

Emily Auerbach

"THE ODYSSEY PROJECT helped me unwrap my gifts and rewrite the story of my life," wrote Terry, a Black single father overcoming incarceration and substance abuse. Told she was "not college material" by a racist high-school guidance counselor and sexually abused by a relative, Char found her voice decades later as she earned her first college credits in the University of Wisconsin–Madison's Odyssey Project: "Odyssey made me feel like a human being, that I existed on earth and had a purpose." How has the Odyssey Project generated transformation not only for Terry and Char but for over five hundred adults overcoming adversity?

When we launched the Odyssey Project in 2003, we had two clear models: the Clemente Course in the Humanities begun by educational reformer Earl Shorris as a way to provide a "great works" course in literature, philosophy, art, and history to low-income adults; and Berea College, a progressive Kentucky school subsidizing a four-year liberal arts education for impoverished students. We also were inspired by the Wisconsin Idea, the belief articulated a century ago that a land-grant university should serve the entire state, not just an elite group of privileged students sitting in traditional college classrooms.

So, are the liberal arts elitist? The twenty-year success of the Odyssey Project points to a paradoxical answer. No, the liberal arts are not elitist because they can be life-changing for anyone. Yes, the liberal arts are elitist because we deny equal access to them.

"Why would poor people want to study William Blake, Shakespeare, and Socrates?" asked a reporter back in 2003. "Don't you think you'll have trouble filling your class?" In fact, over one hundred adults applied for thirty spots in the initial Odyssey Project. They had discovered in the public library, the YWCA, St. Vinnie's, or a homeless shelter an Odyssey flyer announcing, "Begin your journey to college for free." To qualify, students needed to be eighteen, have severe financial need, be able to read a newspaper in English, and be committed to attending evening classes for two semesters. To remove barriers, Odyssey provided free tuition, textbooks, childcare, and transportation, and held classes off campus in a community center serving low-income families.

Each year from September to May Odyssey students engage in lively discussions of a wide range of literary, philosophical, and historical texts and works of art, including poetry by Emily Dickinson, Walt Whitman, Langston Hughes, and Maya Angelou; plays from Shakespeare's *Macbeth* to Lorraine Hansberry's *A Raisin in the Sun*; speeches and essays by Frederick Douglass, Abraham Lincoln, Elizabeth Cady Stanton, Malcolm X, and Martin Luther King Jr.; fiction by Francisco Jiménez, Kate Chopin, and Toni Morrison; and artwork by Leonardo da Vinci, Rembrandt, Romare Bearden, and Frida Kahlo.

Discussing the trial and death of Socrates triggers intense conversations on the value of asking questions ("The unexamined life is not worth living") and the need for integrity in the face of injustice. After reading Charles Dickens's *A Christmas Carol*, students find Ebenezer Scrooge in twenty-first-century Madison: their landlord evicting them in the winter or an ICE official callously deporting them.

How can a metaphor change a life? After reading Plato's Allegory of the Cave, students describe being trapped in their own caves of domestic abuse, religious indoctrination, and narrow-mindedness. After reading metaphorical poetry, students write poems of identity – "I am a volcano, the pain of my childhood making me ready to explode" or "I used to be gravel, but now I am a brick, strong and hard, building foundations that last forever." After viewing famous self-portraits, they represent themselves visually through stark images. For Tracy, depicting herself with markers and a piece of paper saved her life. "I am a person in a revolving door," she said, explaining her picture. "Right when I think I'm about to get out the door, my friends still on drugs drag me back around. There I go again, stuck, never getting out, never going forward." Tracy claims the assignment allowed her to understand her past, present, and future, finally empowering her to end her addiction.

A free college-access program targeting poverty invariably addresses racial inequities. Nearly 95 percent of Odyssey students come from communities of color. Although outsiders view Madison as a liberal and enlightened city, statistics beg to differ. Black, Latino, and Asian

American families in Dane County face higher rates of poverty and lower rates of educational achievement than their Caucasian counterparts. Wisconsin locks up a larger portion of its Black residents than any other state. With our Odyssey Beyond Bars program, we now offer college-credit courses in four Wisconsin prisons, with plans to expand to more correctional institutions as well.

When parents earn college credits through our programs, their children and grandchildren begin thinking of themselves as college bound, breaking cycles of generational poverty. At age eight, Dauntrea, who was in our Odyssey Junior program, first thought about college when her grandmother completed Odyssey; Dauntrea now has a UW bachelor's degree, has completed an internship with the Washington, DC, branch of the NAACP, and has her eyes set on law school.

When Keena applied for the Odyssey Project in 2010, she was homeless and sleeping on the floor of a barbershop. She now has a UW bachelor's degree, businesses of her own, and two sons eyeing college. "Because we were in Odyssey and Odyssey Junior, my sons talk not *if* but *where* they will go to college," Keena says. Other Odyssey graduates have moved from homelessness to bachelor's and master's degrees, from incarceration to meaningful work in the community, from depression to fulfilling self-expression. "I was silenced by life but am learning to find my voice," writes Ericka, a Black mother of four now on her way to a social-work degree.

We must ensure that the liberal arts reach everyone. To do otherwise is not only elitist but unjust.

A History of Liberation

Brandon McCoy

COMMONPLACE IN EDUCATION DISCOURSE is a worry that the liberal arts are on their way out, with some people suggesting their exit might even be good for the world. In a globalized, fast-paced, technology-driven world, some contend there is hardly an excuse to have students secluded in ivory towers contemplating abstract ideas. People assert that their tax dollars, donations, and tuition payments ought to go toward programs that guarantee a positive return on investment by training students to enter the workforce. Even pushing economic considerations aside, many believe that the liberal arts are not worth defending because for centuries they have only been accessible to the upper echelon of society.

The popular rejection of the liberal arts for a more skills-based education is understandable if the liberal arts have not historically been a part of the lives of all people. However, the history of the liberal arts is far from irredeemable.

They have been a source of liberation for downtrodden and subjugated groups and have inspired institutions of equality, such as democracy, and the defense of natural and civil rights.

These claims flow from an honest, comprehensive history of the liberal arts, one that considers this educational model in both a global and American context. Such a history should orient us to today's educational landscape and motivate us to cherish a liberal arts education and work to make it accessible to more people.

A Brief History of Liberal Arts Education

The origins of liberal arts education stretch back to ancient Greece. In their earliest form, the liberal arts were reserved for free people.[1] In ancient Athens, the population was bifurcated between the enslaved and the freemen who enjoyed the rights of citizenship. Early liberal arts education emphasized the importance of the individual. Entrusted with state duties, citizens needed a liberal arts education to discharge these public responsibilities. Roman scholars such as Boethius and Cicero later specified the arts studied by the Greeks, codifying the seven liberal arts: the trivium of grammar, logic, and rhetoric, and the quadrivium of arithmetic, geometry, music, and astronomy. The primary concern of the liberal arts in ancient civilizations was to equip free men to navigate issues related to human flourishing and the common good.[2]

As Europe entered the Middle Ages and Christianity began to take hold in the West, what was considered a liberal arts education shifted to include issues of faith and spirituality. Rather than training men to serve the political community, the primary goal of the liberal arts became to seek knowledge pertaining to God and the church. Christian influences on the liberal arts can be seen in the emphasis during this period on logic over the other humanistic arts – grammar and rhetoric.[3]

From the eleventh to fourteenth centuries, Europe witnessed the emergence and growth of the medieval university. The University of Bologna and the University of Paris were the first, and they became the model for many more places of instruction. The University of Paris became recognized as an important source of interpretation of Catholic doctrine, training scholars such as Thomas Aquinas. Paris included residential colleges where students and a resident master resided. Bologna began as a law school and operated differently from the University of Paris. In Bologna, the students paid teachers, whereas in Paris, the teachers were paid by the church. Therefore, Bologna often permitted more secular studies, per the directive of the students. Oxford and Cambridge later emerged and followed the Paris residential college model. This model would endure, and it would later evolve into the residential college system adopted by many American colleges during the colonial period.[4]

Students in university would receive frequent lectures. As the printing press had not yet been invented, most instruction was oral. Students would be trained in the seven liberal arts. The arts at most of the schools were examined through a Christian lens under the guidance and surveillance of the church. Those who completed the first three arts (the trivium) were bachelors, and those who completed all seven became masters, who would in turn teach the arts to other students.

While Christianity continued to maintain a dominant role in the instruction of the liberal arts, early humanists reformed the model by challenging and broadening the scope of what was studied. Humanists reemphasized the centrality of the individual, which had been more prevalent in the Greco-Roman period. The goals of humanists and of the church often clashed. Humanists' embrace of human nature contrasted with the church's attempts to critique the excesses and shortcomings of human nature.[5] Most of the humanists' momentum was generated outside of the medieval university, and curricula within the institutions were slow to change until 1500.[6] But as humanism gained steam, grammar, not logic, became the most significant of the seven arts.

The shift toward an emphasis on grammar had major ramifications that continue to affect the liberal arts in the present day. First, as the West entered the Renaissance, scholars emphasized learning the ancient languages of Greek and Latin. For scholars and clergy, study of ancient vernacular became central to a liberal education. Second, the humanists during the Renaissance saw studying great authors and books as important to developing knowledge and independent thought.[7]

The development of the United States and its education system underscore general trends experienced across Europe. Early American colonial education continued to be delivered in the liberal arts tradition. Boston Latin School, the country's first public school, grounded its curriculum in the liberal arts.[8] The earliest American colleges also continued instruction in the liberal arts. Until the mid-nineteenth century, the liberal arts remained dominant in higher education.[9]

In the American colonial period and in the early years of the republic, education was reserved for the affluent and powerful. No state mandated enrollment in school until 1852 (Massachusetts), and it would not be until 1918 that every state had such a mandate, so poor and working-class citizens would often only receive a few years of schooling.[10] At the turn of the twentieth century, roughly 6 percent of American youths completed high school, and only 2 percent of young Americans completed a college education.[11]

Influences domestic and foreign caused both the accessibility and purpose of education to shift radically. During the American Civil War, the United States issued a number of land grants to found public colleges and universities. Furthermore, during the Reconstruction Era and afterward, the United States wrestled with how education ought to serve the newly freed Black citizens. Training schools, in large part due to the efforts of Booker T. Washington, were opened throughout the southern states to educate Black men and women to serve as industrial workers, teachers, and agriculturalists, and in other working-class professions.[12] Less common, though still notable, was training in the classical studies of the liberal arts for Black Americans. Scholars and activists such as W. E. B. Du Bois, who stressed the value of liberal arts education for liberation for

Black men, and Anna Julia Cooper, who did the same for Black women, were successful in birthing a class of Black intellectuals who applied the liberal principles embedded in the liberal arts to the fight for civil rights.[13]

During this same time, however, the liberal arts would be challenged by domestic and overseas education movements taking aim at many facets of them. In Prussia (now Germany), an educational model focused on vocational training and civic duty began to spread and caught the attention of many reformers in the United States.[14] Notable Progressive figures such as Horace Mann, John Dewey, and Francis Parker were in part influenced by the Prussian model, and they applied it to the United States' burgeoning public education system. Public school, from kindergarten through high school, aimed to educate a citizenry – not just the landed elites, but its entirety – to become a democratic and productive populace.

Throughout most of the twentieth century, the ideals of these Progressives shaped American education. Today, roughly 90 percent of all K–12 students are in public school.[15] In higher education, one does not need to look far to uncover an emphasis on skills acquisition. The American collegiate model could be generally described as an economic investment: a student pays for courses either out of pocket or through loans in order to become gainfully employed in a specific domain.

Nevertheless, the liberal arts still retain some strong footholds in the American education system. Institutions such as St. John's College adhere to a Great Books program akin to the universities of the late Middle Ages and Renaissance periods.[16] Numerous K–12 charter and private schools have emerged over the past two decades with the purpose of revisiting the classical models of the liberal arts and the humanities. Outside the United States, liberal education models can be found in varying forms in Europe, Asia, and the Middle East.[17]

Elitism for All?

As history indicates, education did not become accessible to the poor and disenfranchised until many of the old institutions safeguarding education were directly challenged, and the purpose of education underwent significant revision. Modern forms of education emerged as the world became freer and more equal. Education became something that was not only more accessible, but also a public right. The ivory tower fell, and with it, supposedly useless studies such as Latin and the classics. According to this view, education, to be for *everyone*, must be practical, guaranteeing each person basic literacy and fundamental competency in math and science, and, most importantly, providing a pathway to a profession.

Indeed, the public enjoys freedoms today that were inaccessible to most in the past, and this is a great development. However, elitism remains in education and society more broadly, even as its form has shifted. Only a minority of students have the privilege of studying the liberal arts and pondering questions of ultimate value and human purpose. While more students attend classes, most merely receive job training, rather than the formation intended to equip them for public service and lives of leisure. The ancient understandings of education operated within a paradox: they stressed the importance of developing free-thinking men while preparing these men to serve and lead the state. Early modern reformers attempted to critique traditional education as unfree and undemocratic, but they ultimately faced the same tension. For example, education reformer Horace Mann echoes the ancients' position on education as liberation, but he too sees the goal of this liberation as service to society:

> In teaching the blind, and the deaf and dumb, in kindling the latent spark of intelligence that lurks in an [intellectually disabled] mind, and in the more holy work of reforming abandoned and outcast children, education has proved what it can do, by glorious experiments. . . . When it shall be trained to wield its mighty energies for the protection of society against the giant vices which now invade and torment it . . . then, there will not be a height to which these enemies of the [human] race can escape, which it will not scale, nor a Titan among them all, whom it will not slay.[18]

Where, then, does the difference between the ancients and the moderns lie? One can look to John Dewey, who built upon the compulsory education concept created by Mann to further education's purpose to promote democracy. It is impossible to disentangle moral education from any mode of instruction, but Dewey differed from Mann by emphasizing collective experience rather than Mann's nonsectarian Christian moralism. Needing a common ethos to preserve the ultimate goal of protecting democracy,

Dewey proclaims "education is a regulation of the process of coming to share in the social consciousness; and the adjustment of individual activity on the basis of this social consciousness is the only sure method of social reconstruction."[19] People assumed truth then as more subjective and practicable rather than objective and knowable.[20] In seeking to make education less directive or coercive, these reformers made it more trivial, even while continuing to smuggle in a vision of the good society.

As a result, philanthropist Eugene M. Lang writes, "curricula have been modified to dilute the European tradition of Platonic idealism with the American tradition of philosophical pragmatism."[21] To be sure, this has not been all negative. As the United States has become more diverse and democratic, its educational institutions have put a greater emphasis on learning more languages, reading and writing more diverse bodies of literature and histories, and responding to the needs of an industrialized economy. Nevertheless, the present system fails to maintain many of the best attributes of liberal education. To meet the needs of a diverse and democratic society, modern education values inclusion and accommodation over universal content and a common human questioning. To meet the needs of an industrialized economy, modern education values specialization over forming students within traditions that explicitly debate and promote transcendent values.

Moreover, modern education has not rid our society of elitism. The bifurcation of paths for people to choose particular careers or professions perpetuates an upper and lower caste rather than establishing a common human foundation for all. Technical or "vocational" training is available for those who wish to learn a skill and enter the workforce upon completion of their training. Ironically, in a system that values meeting the economic demands of today, vocational pathways are derided for being non-academic and low-class.[22] Meanwhile, "elites" attend professional schools to learn non-manual trades. Certainly, these professional trades require critical thinking, but it is a thinking that is better defined as "expertise" than as "wisdom." Regardless of whether one is a doctor, a lawyer, or a plumber, the present-day education system has abandoned a "search for truth" in order to meet "workforce needs."[23]

Given this lack, it is not a surprise that many people and institutions have revived interest in the liberal arts. Both private schools and charter schools have organized their curricula around introducing children to the Great Books and ancient languages. Many of these K–12 schools situated in urban communities serve nearly entirely minority a nd low-income student bodies.[24] At the collegiate level, a variety of scholars have explored the connections between the lessons of antiquity and the flourishing of democracy and justice.[25] As a result, liberal arts formation has been shown to be a catalyst for civic participation and philosophical exploration in both the East and the West.[26]

While productivity and financial security are laudable goals, they should not be the primary purpose of education. The goal of education should be to create liberated persons who seek to examine life in its fullness, to enjoy friendship with others, and to foster the health of their communities. In a modern context, the liberal arts form students to understand themselves as more than their skills or economic value to society. What was once thought of as elite education becomes a universal practice to liberate anyone who desires to pursue these virtues.

Modern Purposes for Ancient Instruction

Our civilization looks very different from the society in which the liberal arts tradition originated. Information is transmitted freely and is more accessible than ever before. While we have not achieved full equality, a continuous pursuit of securing rights for everyone – privileged or otherwise – is paramount in most institutions. There is a near-universal understanding that a democratic society needs an educated citizenry, ready and able to contribute civically.

Since its origins, the liberal arts tradition has centered its purpose on liberating the individual from various kinds of ignorance. In his *Metaphysics*, Aristotle highlights the importance of the pursuit of wisdom, "since it is because of wondering at things that humans, both now and at first, began to do philosophy."[27] Wisdom, while useful for a number of tasks, is valuable in its own right: "we do not inquire into [wisdom] because of its having another use, but just as a human being is free, we say, when he is for his own sake and not for someone else, in the same way we pursue this as the only free science, since it alone is for its own sake."[28] The classics within this tradition continue to provide the starting point for students' intellectual journeys because they speak to our common human condition and to our fundamental aspirations. Cultivating a mind that perpetually seeks knowledge is imaginable when curricula connect students to ideas, endeavors, and challenges of the past, present, and future.[29]

Those invested in the liberal arts should not seek to return to an ancient time. The liberal arts can and must adapt for a society that is more industrialized, democratized, and diverse. Fortunately, this adaptation is both good and possible. In the institutions where it still thrives, liberal arts education has been a strong driver of civic participation. Additionally, the liberal arts are not anathema to a growing economy. Both the medieval universities and the present-day liberal arts colleges train individuals in professions. Where they diverge from career or skills-based forms of education is in their insistence that social or economic utility does not define the worth of a human life. Students trained in the liberal arts may go on to master particular crafts, but within these occupations, they will question how their positions serve ultimate human goods and whether their work is true, good, and beautiful.[30]

The Catherine Project

Zena Hitz

THE PINNACLE OF INTELLECTUAL LIFE, so far as I am concerned, is to sit around a table talking about the deep questions, inspired by an excellent book. We are drawn to that table from a desire to understand and to learn, with and from one another. We read, speak, and listen not to draw a boundary between ourselves and others, but to uncover bonds of human unity.

I had the privilege to attend St. John's College, a small liberal arts college with a similar vision of learning, and I have the privilege of teaching there now. But I dreamt for years of ways to bring to the table anyone who wanted to join in the conversation. I envisioned education without strings attached – no grades, no credits, no tuition, run on the manifest love of learning alone. It took the Covid shutdowns of 2020 to see a way to begin. I began organizing small online tutorials and reading groups via videoconference. I found readers from various backgrounds on Twitter. We began with four tutorials on Homer and two reading groups, one on Aristophanes and one on Kafka. Since then we have hosted groups on Tolstoy, George Eliot, Rilke, Rousseau, Augustine, and Euclid, among others. Late in the fall of 2020, the Kafka group wanted to move on to Kierkegaard, but sought more readers for the difficult endeavor. I posted on Twitter: "Who wants to read

Either/Or on Saturday evenings?" I received more than a hundred messages. We called it "the Kierkegaard explosion" and organized several more groups to accommodate them. One evening last fall we held seminars on the book of Genesis. We filled as many groups as we had leaders for, capping it at seventy readers. The appetite for learning is much larger than the capacities of our little organization.

Great books respond to one another and in doing so form traditions, conversations among the wise over centuries. In the form of helpless books, they cannot refuse us entry. The Catherine Project seeks to introduce readers to the great traditions – European, Near Eastern, African, and Asian, each overlapping with the others. We are too small to take this on systematically, so we harness the enthusiasm of our volunteers and make our way on small tracks, like a snowplow through a great mountain range.

We aspire to the simplicity of the great Christian martyr Catherine of Alexandria, who is reported to have refuted fifty court philosophers with her eloquence. Her modern-day namesake, Catherine Doherty, followed a similar simplicity when she founded the first national lending library in Canada, mailing out donated books into the remotest places on request.

As Doherty discovered, the love of learning is not limited by age, geography, or social class. Our groups are open to anyone free of cost. But they are as intimate as the top programs in world-class universities. Our tutorials are capped at four to six readers, with short weekly writing assignments. We consider our readers to be driven independently by their own questions, and mentor them in developing their own thinking and reading. We frequently teach outside our areas of expertise, which lends our conversations spontaneity and an open-ended character. In addition to our tutorials, we also run peer-led reading groups on various books or topics. These groups are larger – we aim for eight to ten readers – and are more flexible as to their length and structure. Our readers have begun to connect with one another to form their own groups. It would fulfill our dearest hopes to be put out of business in this way.

We work online, through videoconference, as that way we reach people and places where intellectual community is hard to find. We hope in this way to form a network and to discover areas where zealous readers might be concentrated. One day we hope to have physical homes, brick-and-mortar readers' libraries where anyone can come to study and meet others in study. In the meantime, we host three-dimensional gatherings when feasible.

In the world of institutional higher education, humanistic learning is ever more difficult to find. Perhaps institutions will change their tune if movements like ours grow large enough. If not, we help to shape communities that do not depend on the university system alone for their intellectual engagement. Our studies benefit anyone, whatever their career path or lack thereof. Universities are wonderful, but they are not necessary for human flourishing.

The Catherine Project has served over a thousand readers, many of whom study in multiple groups and return term after term. All of our group leaders and tutors are volunteers. We are committed never to charge tuition, and welcome new readers from all walks of life.[31]

Aren't the Liberal Arts Liberal?

The liberal arts are aptly named: liberal arts professors at elite colleges are almost entirely liberal or progressive, and students who attend these institutions often adopt a more progressive political ideology. Liberal arts institutions brainwash students, lead them to abandon their religion, and exacerbate the political polarization that afflicts society.

Respecting Reality

Anne Snyder

THE DRAMATIC PAUSE dared our sophomoric slouches to snap out of it. "Are you ready to delve into the foundation of all reality?" Dr. Wood asked on the first day of Philosophy 101. His eyes were serious, no guile permitting us to laugh. "Here," he said with effect, "is where every question that human beings have ever asked about the nature of truth and our lives in this world is born. We are going to get down to the bottom-most whys."

I can still recall the sensation of intrigue – and also of homecoming – that flooded my being. I had been searching for a thread to sew together a course of study that was starting to resemble a quilt whose pattern I could sense but not explain. Every class invited a conversation with another – politics with sociology, literature with psychology, theology with physics – and one year into this liberal arts experience, most days found me in wonder at how much was connected. I was just missing an articulate thread.

Wood's class compelled me to major in philosophy, but it has since been my experience that almost anyone granted the experience of a liberal arts education – whether they've read Kierkegaard or not – tends to be marked by curiosity about the foundational order of things, an order that we can never completely grasp, but one whose harmonies beckon us always into a quest for understanding, ideally in the company of others.

It has taken me a long time to discern my way to a vocational responsibility that not only continues this quest but invites others into it. So much of my twenties were spent first being perplexed by, and then actively seeking to circumvent, the dulling forces of ideological turf wars and top-down generalizations in an era of elite self-absorption and fraying social bonds. Cutting my professional teeth in Washington, DC, I found much presumption about Americans' lives but little curiosity, and articulate systemic critiques but next to no imaginative capacity. What had happened to some of our best and brightest, that they were so straitjacketed by ideological boundaries and circular questions of identity? And why did I feel so comparatively free?

Fast forward a couple of decades, and I have the joy now of running *Comment*, a magazine that seeks to renew North American social architecture from the wells of two thousand years of Christian social thought. In our essays and gatherings, we zoom in on the norms and institutions that serve as the scaffoldings and skeleton of social life: families and financial systems, politics and education, museums and labor unions, religious communities and neighborhoods. Our mandate is broad, our questions provoked by some of the most concerning trends in the present day: the loss of trust and erosion of friendships, the weakening of institutional authority and the temptations toward tribe, our growing inability to converse peaceably about contested narratives of history, and the atrophy of constructive practice in nearly every arena that is forming young people.

The discipline of the job is to stay humble before harsh and swiftly moving societal currents while hanging on to an overarching vision of the good. My fellow editors and I try to discern the times, study history, and highlight those individual and institutional exemplars that are staking out a healthy way forward, all in hopes of prompting a constant dialogue between macro reflection and self-excavation so our readers are better equipped to serve and to lead. Like a good professor, we don't believe that distanced judgments awaken one's loves. Rather, reality has to be discovered through a process of encounter and exchange – some of it in books and essays, much of it around tables and shared projects.

It is the liberal arts that gave me these instincts, as much through a curriculum as through a relational pedagogy. In an era of dogma and either-or thinking, it's an education that forges powerful question-askers who do not fear tension. At a time when so many people need to make sense of chaos quickly, and charlatan narrators of history pose as prophets, the liberal arts grant the criterion that *human* concerns must stay primary. In a society struggling to manage the seduction of technology, the liberal arts offer a way of thinking and perceiving that no machine will be able to match. And perhaps most lasting, the liberal arts expose us to the breadth of moral sentiments that make it a delicious thing to be human – and a fearsome responsibility too.

Truth U, Justice U, Jesus U

Joseph Clair

COLLEGE AND UNIVERSITY PROFESSORS in the liberal arts (humanities, social sciences, and natural sciences) are almost entirely left-leaning, liberal, or progressive, and this is especially true among faculty in the humanities and social sciences. Insofar as political party affiliation is representative, the statistics are stunning – roughly 12:1 Democrat to Republican in the humanities and social sciences nationally, and this ratio is even more pronounced in certain selective schools (Brown University takes the cake with 60:1).[1] Students who attend liberal arts colleges or universities (that is, non-trade, non-vocational schools that require core curricula and keep an array of majors in the disciplines of the humanities, social sciences, and natural sciences) often adopt more liberal or progressive points of view as a result of their education. There are many great literary depictions of this transformation and the ensuing alienation that often results when such students return home from college. My favorite is in Flannery O'Connor's short story, "Revelation," where a young woman in a doctor's office throws her human development textbook at the unenlightened, uncouth, hometown character Ruby Turpin.[2] Is this phenomenon accidentally related to the demography of the professoriate or somehow intrinsically related to the craft and content of the liberal arts themselves and the culture and atmosphere of the campus?

Despite frequently being casually conflated, the terms "liberal" and "progressive" represent different political traditions in the West, and when applied to the liberal arts represent different approaches to education. "Liberal" liberal arts education represents a modern vision of the disciplines oriented toward an Enlightenment-style view of objective truth pursued by rational and empirical methods, whereas "progressive" is often associated today with postmodern visions of education that are suspicious of privileged categories such as knowledge, truth, and understanding. Progressive liberal arts education is aimed toward dismantling systems of illegitimate power and ensuring equality of outcomes for all. Melded with this mission of social justice is a corresponding emphasis on trauma and the paradoxes and slipperiness of selfhood and identity.

NYU social psychologist Jonathan Haidt argues that these two visions of the liberal arts are ultimately incompatible, and that universities ought to be forced to make a choice between the aims of objective truth and social justice, and organize academic life accordingly.[3] Haidt creates a helpful typology, calling the "liberal" approach "Truth U" and the progressive approach "Social Justice U."

He notes that almost every major liberal arts institution in America today has become a Social Justice U, by default of the demography of the professoriate. One notable exception is the University of Chicago, with its classically liberal commitments enshrined in its "Chicago Principles" on academic freedom.[4]

Haidt notes that some religious colleges in America present themselves as pursuing an entirely different telos, or guiding goal, altogether, outside of his binary framework. Haidt points to Wheaton College in Illinois as an example whose mission is explicitly to "serve Jesus Christ and advance His Kingdom." Haidt calls this exceptional case "Jesus U" and does not seem to take it seriously. Haidt is committed to his own liberal, Enlightenment-style vision of the liberal arts, inspired by the classical liberalism of J. S. Mill.

To answer the question of whether the liberal arts are inherently liberal or progressive requires that we first tease apart the liberal and progressive adaptations of liberal education. Haidt's dichotomy of Truth U and Social Justice U helpfully encapsulates the difference between them. Both the liberal and progressive approaches to the liberal arts retain something essential from the earlier tradition but both deviate significantly from the classical and Christian view of the human person that gave birth to the earliest universities and liberal arts colleges in Europe and America. The "liberal" liberal arts approach of Truth U retains the classical and fundamental insistence on the connection between intellectual cultivation and citizenship, yet it abandons the transcendent framework by which truth-pursuit can be understood as an expression of our deepest human telos. The progressive approach of Social Justice U retains something essential from the specifically Christian insistence on the connection between liberal learning and neighbor-love, yet it abandons the redemptive vision the Christian story brings to critiques of power, care for victims, and confession of sin.

For these reasons, we ought to take Christian liberal arts institutions more seriously than Haidt does. Such a model is a viable alternative to the liberal or progressive adaptations of the liberal arts on offer today. This tradition is capacious enough to be appealing to Christians and non-Christians alike, and is adaptable to other religious or philosophical approaches that do not fit neatly into either the liberal or progressive approaches to the liberal arts. The Christian university of the twenty-first century ought to present a picture of the human person and the role of intellectual cultivation in human flourishing that transcends the impasse of liberal and progressive approaches to the liberal arts.

Truth U, or the "Liberal" Liberal Arts

The ancient Greco-Roman view of the liberal arts was associated with the special status of being a free person (*liber*) rather than a servant or slave (*servus*) – a *servus* was a person for whom training in the manual or mechanical (servile) arts was most fitting. Free people needed the intellectual agility and capacity for thought and communication embedded in the *liber*-al arts to participate in free, self-governing societies. The liberal arts are by definition liberalizing – they make someone more suited for citizenship in a free society and intellectually agile enough to engage a variety of viewpoints with subtlety and generosity. The ancient founders of the liberal arts could not have imagined the modern American attempt to extend this vision to include all human beings (including women, slaves, foreigners, et al.) on the scale of a democratic republic with over three hundred million citizens. The slow unfolding of civil rights and the expansion of the liberal arts have worked in tandem in American democracy. Yet this project is now under attack from many angles: ideological differences threaten to shatter our ideals, values, and shared sense of the past; general education in the liberal arts evaporates in an effort to hasten time to completion and decrease cost and student debt; career orientation erodes the numbers of students willing to major in liberal arts disciplines.

Christians have historically prized the liberal arts – whether in their classical form as the trivium (grammar, logic, and rhetoric) and quadrivium (geometry, arithmetic, music, and astronomy) or their modern disciplinary expression as the humanities, social sciences, and natural sciences – as being in the whole community's interest and related to our common humanity as divine-image bearers. So both the original Greco-Roman vision and the Christian adaptation of it presume a certain picture of the human person as a creature for whom intellectual cultivation and leisure are fitting.

The true telos of liberal arts education in this sense is happiness, and this connection between education and happiness is the foundation of any such education. But today's "liberal" approach to the liberal arts excludes this connection in principle by relegating metaphysical and theological inquiry to the realm of private belief and individual preference.

What sort of content – what meaningful stories and symbols and corresponding practices and habits – is necessary to animate and contextualize the acquisition of these arts? Truth U's curricula are often simply too spare, too shorn of a transcendent or religious sense of the human person to provide the meaningful context for the disciplinary pursuit of truth. Truth U models all the liberal arts according to the successful techniques of the sciences and exudes a fixation with truth as a kind of methodological rigor – a case in which the natural sciences are masters and social sciences expert imitators, but which punts on fundamental questions of morality and religion that could guide the overall direction of inquiry.[5]

Truth in a purely objective, universal, or rational sense is too bare a telos for the liberal arts to sustain themselves. Rather, they thrive in narrative webs of meaning – of words and images that come freighted with sense and value and hold capacity for shaping worldviews and affections. Christians living in late antiquity saw that part of the task of the Christian educator would be the challenge of migrating the liberal arts tools from their classical Greco-Roman context to a biblical one – which included an exotic new set of stories, characters, ideals, values, images, and emotions – in order to create a Christian culture of liberal education.

Augustine of Hippo (AD 354–430) sensed the conflict between the classical and biblical texts and worked tirelessly to identify the resonance and dissonance among them.[6] Augustine was keen to highlight the common human inheritance of the liberal arts and the inherent dependence of these tools on the world of textual meaning in which they can be acquired and on which they can be practiced. In Augustine's view the classical world comes into direct conflict with the biblical world, and the liberal arts are repurposed in service of the new. He baptized the narrative world of classical culture and embedded it in an alternative story in pursuit of a different god.[7] Slowly the old myths and gods were burned away. Centuries later, as the Enlightenment gave birth to a new vision of liberal arts education in modernity, it returned the favor and slowly banished metaphysics and Christian theology from the list of properly scientific disciplines.

The liberal model of liberal arts education admirably retains the central vision of these arts as the common tools of intellectual agility necessary for an intelligent, free, self-governing society, but it fails to provide a guiding web of shared meaning. It appears impotent to resist the common and reductive vision of education, and of the human person, as defined narrowly by work or material success. It appears unable to gather culture and sustain moral energy around the liberal notion of scientific "truth" as a sacred value. This leaves the students of Truth U vulnerable to a flattened existence, vacillating between materialistic meaninglessness or relativistic consumption of meaning. Truth U's best bet for regaining this energy would be to return to the classical paganism or Christian theology of predecessor models of liberal education, in which the telos of truth is embedded in a more robust world of meaning.

Social Justice U, or the Progressive Liberal Arts

The progressive model of the liberal arts is statistically the most dominant today. The movement of radical 1960s intellectual life into the mainstream of higher education through professional research in the humanities and social sciences over the past half-century is an intriguing and complex historical and sociological tale. One simple way to understand Social Justice U's intellectual framework, however, is as an uneasy alliance between the deconstructive criticism of Friedrich Nietzsche and the Marxist insistence on equality.

Social Justice U's advantage over Truth U is that this uneasy alliance has created a captivating web of meaning in which the tools of the liberal arts can be acquired and tested in social criticism and activism. The critical Nietzschean insight of Social Justice U is the deconstruction of the telos of "truth" in the modern liberal university – critiquing the way "truth" has functioned as a "mobile army of metaphors," a coded expression of the will to dominate others, rooted in privilege, exclusion, and elitism.[8] The irony, however, is that Nietzsche's shrewd analysis of power is rooted in pure historicism and relativism – a rejection of any metaphysical foundation for one's understanding of reality. This leaves one teetering on the brink of nihilism. Recognition of truth as nothing more than expressions of the will to power in the form of education, for Nietzsche, was not cause for lamentation but rather cause for celebrating the naturalness and inevitability of such dominance.

This deconstructive project of unmasking the will to power is then yoked with a secularized version of the Christian instinct for social justice. Social Justice U provides an education in which one is unable to decide between Martin Luther King Jr.'s beloved community or the armed resistance of Malcolm X and the Black Panthers. This choice perfectly highlights the trouble with critiques of power and social injustice without a larger moral framework and imagination to guide the work of education.

This fusion of Nietzschean deconstruction and Marxist transformation could be understood as post-Christian. A latent Christian pathos still provides the necessary moral energy to motivate academic labor despite the loss of a broader web of narrative meaning to make sense of the practice of liberal arts education. The inner logic of unmasking power and defending the victim becomes a totalizing narrative; it is an alternative system of moral authority with unlimited resources for motivation and practice. It is therefore much more suited to replace the medieval and early modern Christian liberal arts university than Truth U.

The success of the moral energy of Social Justice U is rooted in its insistence on the inherent connection between intellectual work and social concern – an evolution of the Christian perspective on the liberal arts that yokes the intellectual and practical goals of education together under the twin commandments of love for God and love for neighbor. In this vision, the professionalization of undergraduate education allows one to make change in the world through practical application. The progressive approach retains the Christian insistence on neighbor-love, even when it rejects the undergirding redemptive vision Christianity offers.

The Christian University as a Viable Alternative

Only by recovering a broader conception of the human person and the way education plays a role in forming such a person can the liberal arts move beyond the impasse between Truth U and Social Justice U. Neither telos – truth or justice – is coherent apart from this broader conception. The Augustinian Christian tradition (at the root of both the medieval Catholic and early modern Protestant vision of the liberal arts) represents one such anthropology and consensus about the web of content in which the tools of the liberal arts gain their coherence and on which they are to be practiced. Of course, there are many Christian traditions and other religious traditions (Jewish, Islamic, and Mormon, for example) in which the big story and anthropology work differently. The commonality of these forms of inquiry shaped by a religious tradition is that they are premised on a picture of a human being (anthropology) and an authoritative set of religious texts read in relation to, and in tension with, the tradition of the liberal arts – in both their ancient origins and modern disciplinary extensions.

The modern secular university's commitment to quantitative methods and techniques of empirical analysis as the highest form of inquiry makes it impossible to rationally justify any non-empirically verified telos whatsoever, whether truth or social justice, for an institution or an individual. The most that can be said is that such teloi are historically dominant and the choice of one over the other is a matter of preference. The Christian university must convincingly reconceive its own work of liberal arts education in light of its own anthropology and the unfolding dialogue between its authoritative texts and the rival or competing texts of the Western liberal arts tradition and other religious or moral traditions. The liberal arts educator in this setting has a double role – both preserving a particular religious framework and engaging rival standpoints to see what's wrong with them and to test one's own tradition.[9] The Christian university can proceed methodologically by what Alasdair MacIntyre calls a "tradition-shaped" form of inquiry, whereby one's own religious perspective is sharpened by liberal arts education and brought into meaningful dialogue and conflict with rival answers to the deepest human questions.

The telos of Jesus U is love. Here the love of learning is tethered to love for God, love for neighbor, and a healthy self-love. Here is a vision of education that eclipses any purely material view of human personality. The social-science caricature of the human person found in both Truth U and Social Justice U amounts to a reduction of human desire to either bare economic self-interest or raw social power. Neither gets to the true depth of human personality. Each appeals to the language of psychology (whether as trauma or happiness) at key moments to get out of the flattened secular horizon and move into the realm of true meaning. Although the social sciences are supposedly methodologically immune to value judgments, they slide into them through the quantitative language of material well-being. This leaves the student hostage to the contested visions of selfhood and identity on offer in the digital coliseum and marketplace. In the Christian vision, self-love is not reducible to economic self-interest or social dominance but recognized as the divine impulse through which one matures and meets the world not as one's oyster but as one's neighbors. The ember of self-love fuels an outward-driving process of moral formation. This view is not reducible to social competition or cooperation but presumes a depth and purpose for liberal education that always exceeds the sum of its parts.

In the Christian university, then, liberal education is brought toward a transcendent horizon that exceeds any purely secular view of political society. Here, citizenship is twofold: One part is committed to the proximate justice and common interest of whatever earthly political situation one finds oneself in. Such political situations are judged from the perspective of the Christian conception of the human person as dignified bearer of the divine image. Justice depends upon a political society's ability to institutionally sustain recognition of this dignity. The other part of citizenship longs for a deeper, truer form of community found in that "eternal city" foreshadowed in the civic images of the Psalms, the Book of Hebrews, and Revelation. Liberal arts education is inherently linked to the formation of new citizens, and thus Christian education imbues citizens with a shrewd sensitivity to the limits of politics. Christians ought to be fiercely loyal to local forms of community *and* fiercely global in outlook, given the history and mission of the church. This produces a kind of spiritual restlessness that resists the temptations of nationalism and goes on pilgrimage.

What would it look like to build a liberal arts institution oriented toward this telos today? It would require a collaborative multidisciplinary team of faculty to work out a new-yet-old vision of truth, and a corresponding epistemological framework that moves beyond the fragmentation of knowledge found in the modern university. It would need to order its community's life around the habits and practices necessary to sustain the marriage of learning and love for God and neighbor. It would need to nurture the character traits – intellectual, moral, and spiritual – most conducive to authentic liberal education. It would need sensitivity to the form and atmosphere of the campus, and creativity in bringing it into harmony with the intellectual and moral aims of the community. Questions about online learning and career preparation might press upon us. But such questions should not distract from more basic ones. We should be encouraged that educational endeavors in the Christian liberal arts tradition have emerged and succeeded in much less auspicious times than our own.

Elite Education for the Rest of Us

John Mark Reynolds

IMAGINE AN ELITE HIGH-SCHOOL EDUCATION in the liberal arts, structured around one-on-one tutorials, offered to anyone regardless of ability to pay. We no longer have to imagine, thanks to a growing movement of schools offering classical education to students of all ages. I have the privilege of teaching every day at one such school, the Saint Constantine School and College in Houston, Texas. Here, nobody is turned away based on financial ability.

A student came to us from another country with no English, started a classical education at our school, graduated from our high school with honors, and ended up in a major university. Another student came into our college-level program burdened with debt from other higher education institutions and graduated without borrowing another dollar, having received an education through one-on-one tutorials and small group discussions.

A classical education prioritizes teachers and students. Just as Constantine could think outside old ideas, imagining a renewed classical Rome without the dying city itself, so a classical educator today can dispense with old categories and find new structures for schooling. For example, our primary, middle, and high school programs and faculty are fully integrated with the college. This enables everyone to teach at any level, expanding opportunity and cutting costs. The opportunity to teach on several levels destroys the implicit hierarchy that respects college educators more than other teachers. This also brings efficiency in certain highly specialized areas, such as mathematics and the sciences, where both college and high school programs can be expensive if artificially separated.

The high cost of administration causes many schools to be unable to pay teachers what they deserve. That is why our school demands that every administrator teach. As a result, teachers make the decisions, and the maximum amount of funds goes to the classroom. This is made possible by the generosity of our donors and by those families who can afford to pay full tuition. Our community has chosen students and teachers over any other cost. The campus is simple, repurposing old office buildings prudently so we can serve more students.

These strategies and priorities flow naturally out of the combination of a classical and Christian education. The dialectic, the Socratic question, is the heart of classical education and wonders about *anything and everything*. The Christian begins in the wonder of the revelation of God in Jesus Christ and God's love for all humankind.

The School and College is Orthodox but hires Orthodox, Catholic, and Protestant faculty. An Orthodox bishop once cautioned our leadership not to refer to the Orthodox as "the home team" but as hosts of an educational feast. All students are welcome, regardless of religious commitments, if they will abide by the behavior code of the community. All can bring special dishes to the meal, and all can partake.

This generosity was exemplified by the founding of the University of Balam and by Antiochian Patriarch Ignatius IV in 1988. During a time of sectarian civil war in Lebanon, the patriarch started a university that would serve all the communities of Lebanon. The Orthodox way is to educate all. After all, Orthodox classical education began with Saint Basil urging students to find virtue in pagan Homer. As a result, our school fears no idea or text: we are, in the words we sing in the school troparion, a "city kept in safety for all time." Perfect love casts out academic fears.

As a result of this history, at Saint Constantine the canon is both rooted and expanding. It begins in texts and ideas that are necessary to understanding the history of the church, particularly the Greek culture and language of the New Testament. We also live as citizens of a nation, the United States, with its languages and literature. But the church is global and the languages, literature, and legacy of that global community count too. Our canon and curriculum are formed from these three values: Christian, rooted, and global. This leads to readings and discussions that move naturally from Aksum, Alexandria, Antioch, and Athens to America. We study in Arabic, Latin, Greek, Spanish, and English and are eager to add more languages.

Our school, like many of the new classical schools, is urban by choice so we can include students from many nations and peoples. That's why we started in Houston, one of America's most diverse cities. As our diversity increases, our curriculum grows and changes so all our students can find their roots and their best future selves.

Aren't the Liberal Arts Racist?

The liberal arts tradition is irretrievably complicit in Western colonialism and racism. The "great books" tend to be by white authors, many of whom had very problematic views and practices. Is this really the legacy we want to pass on?

Inside Nyansa Classical Community

Angel Adams Parham

NYANSA CLASSICAL COMMUNITY was founded to bring classical learning and literature to young people of diverse backgrounds who are unlikely to be introduced to this tradition in any other way. Because much of our work has been with children of African descent, it was important to us early on to weave together the classics with the history and culture of Black authors and artists. We have taken great joy in the results. Three moments in particular stand out as I reflect on our work over the past seven years.

The first was at the gala we held in 2017 to introduce friends and donors to our work. My college-student assistants had worked hard to assemble beautiful examples of the artwork the children had done that year as we read Homer's *Odyssey*. What makes this work so compelling for me is that it combines two traditions: the classical tradition of Homer and his great epics and the Black intellectual and artistic traditions. In this case, the children created collage art in the style of Romare Bearden's *Black Odyssey* – a beautiful series which recasts Homer's *Odyssey* by telling the story of African and African-diaspora people in our various journeys across the ocean and in the new places we call home. Bearden, an African American painter of the

Harlem Renaissance, brings a beauty and mastery to this work that is a wonder to behold and a treasure to pass down to new generations.

The second moment was the finale of a series of events which culminated in a trip for several of our students selected to attend a luncheon at Melba's Restaurant in New Orleans. They were being honored for the poetry book they composed in 2019. A talented college student, Josslyn Littles, had created beautifully reimagined black and brown images of the Greek gods and goddesses we had been reading about all year. After reading a story associated with one of the gods, the children would work with their college tutors to write haiku poems that condensed some aspect of that deity's character into only three lines. Then Josslyn gathered the artwork and poetry together to compile a beautiful booklet, which we continue to treasure. Melba's Restaurant bought one hundred copies of the booklet and invited the children to a lunch where they signed the booklets and gave them away to patrons who lined up to receive a copy. It was a powerful moment for the children, seeing that their hard work during the year was paying off in such a tangible way. Their faces glowed and their pride was evident as they basked in the approval of the many adults awaiting their signed copy of the booklet.

After operating as an afterschool program for six years, the Nyansa program came to a halt with the Covid pandemic. We used this time to reassess and reorganize, deciding to distill all that we had been teaching into a formalized curriculum divided into twenty weeks. This would make it possible for others to replicate the best of what we had been practicing since we began our work. It was quite a process! Writers and artists drew together to describe on the page what we had been experiencing in person. This first curriculum – there are more to come – was at the elementary-school level, organized around the cultivation of virtue. This focus on virtue is an apt way to encourage young people in new Nyansa programs to live out our mission.

By the fall of 2021, we were in a position to pilot the curriculum at several different sites. Over the course of the academic year it was used in two schools in Virginia and one in Uganda. One of the most gratifying reports, though, came from Sarah, a teacher who, on her own time after school, took on the challenge of working with two brothers, fifteen and twelve, who were in academic trouble. Even though the material was pitched at an elementary school audience, Sarah was able to use it to break through in learning with the fifteen-year-old, who was behind in reading and exhibited little interest in school. She drew on Nyansa's story-rich curriculum – in addition to Greek mythology, there are Bible stories and Aesop fables – to engage him. Following each story were writing assignments based on the literature that helped to reinforce areas of reading, spelling, and writing with which he had been struggling. The younger brother, for his part, was most attracted to the art project based on African American artist Jacob Lawrence's *Migration* series. All of these lessons integrate literature, history, and art, and we encourage hands-on artwork to stimulate the children's creativity and engagement with the material. The twelve-year-old loved the art, and the stories behind Lawrence's art allowed Sarah to draw this young student into conversations about virtue and vice and consider how to cultivate the one while fleeing from the other.

It has been one of the singular joys of my life to introduce young people – including my own daughters, who participated in Nyansa – to these great literary and artistic traditions. While we would love for every child to benefit from a classic liberal arts education from a young age, this is unlikely to happen any time soon. Nyansa is nimble and can travel to where young people are, whether in a living room after school, working with a tutor, or at a school in urban Virginia or rural Uganda. We are grateful to be part of passing on this great tradition and helping young people find their voices so they can join this millennia-long conversation.

An Expansive Collection

Angel Adams Parham

WHILE IT IS TRUE that there have always been ways of framing the liberal arts in a racially exclusive manner, the tradition itself has always been richer and more diverse than many of its opponents – and adherents – recognize. Those who oppose widespread study of the canonical literature at the core of the liberal arts tradition often do so because they have been misled by adherents of the tradition who have portrayed it too narrowly. These adherents, well-meaning though they may be, make the case that the works of the canon are for everyone, but they often present the texts in isolation, shorn off from the many other voices that have also been part of this great conversation stretching across millennia. We best position ourselves to capture the built-in diversity of the liberal arts tradition when we think in terms of crossroads and conversations. Because the area I know best is Africa and its diaspora, this will be our focus, though there are many other places and cultures which could as easily be the center of the discussion.

Learning at the Crossroads of the Liberal Arts Tradition

The heart of the Western tradition of liberal arts education can be located at the Mediterranean crossroads. A map according to the ancient historian Herodotus, about 440 BC, would include Europe, Asia, Arabia, Libya, Ethiopia, Egypt, and India.[1] These places and their diverse peoples were central to the histories Herodotus discusses in his work, because Greeks in antiquity were well acquainted with these places and their people. When we think in terms of crossroads, we don't study specific literatures and histories in isolation from each other; rather, we read them together in context.

If, for instance, we are studying the literature and society of the ancient world, the culture and literature of the Egyptians should be as central as that of the Greeks – given the imprint of Egypt on the ancient world. The Greek world borrowed from the Egyptians, who had a complex, formidable civilization that had lasted for several millennia before the heyday of ancient Greece. Herodotus had glowing praise for the learning of the Egyptians:

> As far as human matters are concerned, the priests all agreed in what they told me. They claimed that the Egyptians were the first people to discover the year, and to distribute throughout the year the twelve parts into which they divided the seasons. . . . It seems to me that the Egyptian

monthly system is cleverer than the Greek one: the progress of the seasons forces the Greeks to insert an intercalary
month every other year, whereas because the Egyptians have
twelve months of thirty days and add five extra days on to
every year, the seasonal cycle comes round to the same point
in their calendar each time.[2]

This is one example among many that point toward the
influence of ancient Egypt on many parts of the world.
And we should not limit ourselves to written texts when
studying the influence of Egypt on the Mediterranean
world. There are many excellent resources for studying its
history, literature, and culture through a combination of
text, artifacts, and images.[3]

In addition to studying the place of Egypt at the
crossroads of antiquity, Ethiopia and Ethiopians should
also be studied, given their cultural and symbolic significance in the ancient world. First, it is important to know
that when ancient writers spoke of "Ethiopians" they
generally meant dark-skinned Africans who may or may
not have been from the place that we call Ethiopia today.
Homer and other Greek writers understood Ethiopia to be
a place of beauty and plenty, as is clear in this passage from
Book I of the *Odyssey*:

At length their rage the hostile powers restrain,
All but the ruthless monarch of the main.
But now the god, remote, a heavenly guest,
In Ethiopia grac'd the genial feast....
There on the world's extremest verge, rever'd
With hecatombs and pray'r in pomp prefer'd,

Distant he lay; while in the bright abodes
Of high Olympus Jove conven'd the gods.[4]

The passage speaks of Poseidon, who was the "monarch of
the main [sea]" and was alone among the gods in exercising
wrath toward Odysseus while the rest of the gods met in
Olympus. After causing trouble for Odysseus, Poseidon
retreated to Ethiopia, where he feasted on hecatombs – the
meat of sacrificed animals – and immersed himself in the
pomp and comfort provided by his Ethiopian hosts.[5]

This favorable impression of Ethiopians is much the
same when Herodotus writes of a delegation to them from
the Persian king Cambyses. Cambyses had determined
that he could take the Carthaginians straightforwardly
by sea, and the Ammonians by land. But the Ethiopians
were quite another matter. For this fabled group, he sensed
that he would need a more subtle approach. So rather
than attacking directly, he sent emissaries from an ethnic
group called the Fish-Eaters. These Fish-Eaters had the
secret mission of acting as spies to determine the best way
to defeat the Ethiopians. Here is a bit from Herodotus'
account. Note how the Ethiopians are portrayed, and
remember that though these are not necessarily the people
of today's country of Ethiopia, they were dark-skinned
African people:

> [Cambyses] gave [the Fish-Eaters] gifts to take, including a
> purple cloak, a gold torque, arm-bands, an alabaster pot of
> perfume, and a jar of palm wine. The Ethiopians in ques-
> tion, the ones to whom Cambyses sent the delegation, are
> said to be the tallest and most attractive people in the world.[6]

The Fish-Eaters relayed Cambyses' message to the Ethiopian king, saying that they were sent with gifts because Cambyses desired to be his friend. But the king was no fool. He unmasked their real purpose and then proceeded to deride the gifts they had brought, arguing that – other than the wine – the Ethiopians could produce better, more impressive goods and gifts. He then prepared a message of his own, threatening to come take Cambyses down with his men if he didn't desist from trying to take over land that was not his.

The emissaries were awed and sought to better understand the Ethiopians' culture and ways of living. The king told them that Ethiopians lived up to 120 years. When the Fish-Eaters expressed surprise, the king took them to a special place, and here is what they saw:

> The king took them to a spring whose water made anyone washing in it more sleek, as if it had been olive oil, and which gave off a scent like violets. In their report, the spies said that the water of this spring was so soft that nothing could float on it, not wood or even anything lighter than wood. . . . Assuming the truth of the reports of this water, it would explain why these Ethiopians are long-lived, if they use it for everything. Then they left the spring and were taken to a prison, where all the prisoners were shackled with golden chains.[7]

Of course the story is fantastical, and many times Herodotus himself is careful to distinguish between what he saw himself and what others told him, and he does not hesitate to say that some things are unbelievable. In this particular case, he is unsure, but suggests that it might be true because the water would help to explain the mystery of Ethiopians' long lives. But the account itself does not need to be strictly factual for it to convey the reality of the Greeks' perceptions and imagination of these dark-skinned Ethiopians. Far from assuming that they were ugly or unworthy because they were dark, the perception was that they were nearly superhuman, and that they lived in a place overflowing with wealth and plenty.

About eight hundred years later, around AD 400, texts record the establishment of the church in Ethiopia. A holistic liberal arts education which includes reading the *Odyssey* and learning about views of Ethiopia in that literature could then study Ethiopia on its own terms by learning of the Ethiopian church through studying its history and the many beautiful paintings, buildings, and religious objects coming from that culture. This is a history and material culture rarely explored by students in Western schools, but for those interested the resources are readily accessible.

Another understudied aspect of history is the incredible cultural influence moving from East to West through the works of Muslim philosophers writing in Arabic between approximately AD 700 and 1400. There is also the influence of Indian mathematicians on Western Europe. While there is insufficient space here to do justice to their many contributions, there are ample resources available to learn and share this history.[8]

None of these African and Eastern contributions to the Mediterranean crossroads are insignificant – they are major contributions that, despite their cultural significance, have nevertheless received little attention in K–12 lesson plans or the general education requirements of most liberal arts colleges and universities. This is why when we think of the "classics" or of writings of the "canon," it is generally people and works of European descent or origin that come to mind. But this is not the way it has to be. And of course this wide-ranging conversation continues into the modern world, and helps us see the liberal arts as a conversation among diverse interlocutors.

The Liberal Arts Tradition as a Conversation

As we enter the modern world, particularly beginning in the eighteenth century, we benefit from a larger number of texts written by people of African descent who enter into the Western conversation on the meaning of existence and the definition of the good we strive for in our lives.[9] This engagement among writers across the centuries is often called the Great Conversation.[10] In the United States, the dawning of what is generally referred to as the Black intellectual tradition is regularly placed at the 1773 publication of Phillis Wheatley's book *Poems on Various Subjects, Religious and Moral*.[11] Wheatley and other writers of the Black intellectual tradition engage vigorously in discussion regarding what it means to be human, the nature of freedom, what it means to be educated, and many other questions central to the liberal arts.

Wheatley is an especially good writer to begin with when it comes to addressing the question: "Aren't the liberal arts racist?" She was kidnapped from her African home at the tender age of about seven years, then received a liberal arts education, including Latin. She was also introduced to and accepted the Christian faith. For many years, Wheatley was shunned by Black scholars who thought of her as an assimilationist who shared white Americans' negative views of blackness. This, however, is a gross misunderstanding of Wheatley, her life, and her work. The misconception is due, no doubt, to the fact that her most anthologized poem is "On Being Brought from Africa to America," from which many readers take her to be saying that she is grateful to have been "saved" from pagan Africa and brought to Christian America. But there is a poetic ambiguity in the phrasing of the poem that allows for a different reading. The full text reads:

> 'Twas mercy brought me from my *Pagan* land,
> Taught my benighted soul to understand
> That there's a God, that there's a *Saviour* too:
> Once I redemption neither sought nor knew.
> Some view our sable race with scornful eye,
> "Their colour is a diabolic die."
> Remember, *Christians*, *Negros*, black as *Cain*,
> May be refin'd, and join th' angelic train.[12]

In the last two lines, she could be saying "Remember (white) Christians, Negros (who are) black as Cain" can also be saved. But she could also be saying "Remember that Christians (whoever they are), (and) Negros (those spiritually) black as Cain" can all be saved. Regardless, the poem finds skin color a superficial difference and that the state of one's soul – including those souls that treat their fellow humans unjustly – is the crucial difference. All of this said, Wheatley did share, with others of her time, the idea that Christianity was superior to all other forms of belief.

Anyone reading the larger corpus of Wheatley's work will soon realize that the negative reading of blackness and Africans so long imputed to her cannot be reconciled with her other poetic and epistolary writings. In a letter exchange with Native American minister Samson Occom, she commiserates with Occom, thanking him for supporting her in advocating for the dignity of her people. In that same letter, she excoriates white Christians for their treatment of Black people, clarifying that she sees them as hypocritical in their ability to espouse Christianity while at the same time denigrating Black people. Expressing her outrage, Wheatley writes:

> In every human Breast, God has implanted a Principle, which we call Love of Freedom; it is impatient of Oppression, and pants for Deliverance; and by the Leave of our Modern Egyptians I will assert, that the same Principle lives in us. God grant Deliverance in his own way and Time, and get him honor upon all those whose Avarice impels them to countenance and help forward the Calamities of their Fellow Creatures.[13]

Wheatley insists here that desire for freedom is a God-given longing and that all are entitled to freedom from enslavement. She points to white Americans as "Modern Egyptians," alluding to the ways the ancient Egyptians oppressed and enslaved the people of Israel in the

Hebrew scriptures. There is nothing to suggest that she has unquestioningly accepted her own inferiority vis à vis white Americans.

In short, Phillis Wheatley was not whitewashed by her classical liberal arts education and her acceptance of Christian faith. Quite the contrary – her education and faith empowered her to use her own mind and to observe truths about oppression and liberation that many white Americans were not eager for her or other Black people to recognize.

Over and over again we witness a similar process at work among writers of the Black intellectual tradition who have read classic works or received a classic liberal arts education. We discern this inheritance in Frederick Douglass, who learned to read and to speak with excellence by surreptitiously reading the *Columbian Orator*, an anthology of classic speeches and dialogues meant to be used in the education of young white boys.[14] We find it in the life of W. E. B. Du Bois, who gained a full liberal arts education in high school, complete with the Greek and Latin languages. His work masterfully combines the history and culture of African American life with many allusions to classic and canonical literature.[15] Anna Julia Cooper is another Black writer and educator who believed that liberal arts education was for everyone, especially recently emancipated Black Americans. In her 1930 speech "On Education" she says:

> Certain studies, certain courses, certain exercises have been tested, tried, accepted by the experience of centuries in the steady progress of humanity. Teachers from Aristotle to the present have sifted and analyzed the various branches of

learning to get at their relative worth as educative factors.
The results of their experiments and analyses are not hidden
in dark places. They are universally accepted by teachers and
thinkers as a reasonable and proper basis for the education
of mankind. The only way to meet those skeptics who still
ask with a half sneer "What is the use of this or that study
for Negroes?" is with the query "Is it good for men?"[16]

There could hardly be a more definitive statement of the
importance of liberal education for all people, and especially for the historically oppressed. This advocacy of
a classical liberal arts education for Black people has
continued into the twentieth and twenty-first century. An
example of this is Marva Collins, who taught her African
American students in Chicago according to a curriculum
teeming with classic works. These children, who came
from communities that struggled a great deal, excelled
greatly, and Collins was catapulted to national and international recognition for her work.[17] In the twenty-first
century, Dr. Anika Prather and I continue the work in the
community and in our writing.[18] And organizations such
as The Odyssey Project and Act Six work to carry out this
educational vision.

IN SUM, OUR ANSWER to the question "Aren't the liberal
arts racist?" is a definitive no. While they can be slanted or
framed in ways that are racially exclusive, such framing is
not integral to what the liberal arts are. Rather, the liberal
arts are capacious enough to embrace multiple peoples and
cultures across time and place, integrating them into a
Great Conversation that spans the ages. In a powerful essay

entitled "Of Cannons and Canons," professor Oludamini Ogunnaike argues that now, more than ever, what is needed is literacy in the liberal arts rooted in study of the canon.[19] Ogunnaike is especially well positioned to address this question of the imputed racism of the liberal arts in the Western tradition because he comes from post-colonial Nigeria and has been witness to the deep debates roiling post-colonial circles about the potential harms and benefits of Western education. He eloquently describes our current situation when he explains that "what we generally have are educational systems that teach neither the Western tradition nor any other tradition nor even critical thinking. They have become very good at training students in particular practical and technical skills and techniques, but what they have produced is a bumper crop of 'wizards without wisdom.'" The solution? Train students to be fluent in more than one canonical tradition, so that they can see how traditions speak to each other and be better positioned to understand both their own and others' traditions. Liberal arts may pave the path to wisdom. Greater mutual understanding and respect requires more, not less, education in the liberal arts for everyone.

How to Fight Over the Canon

Jonathan Tran

WHICH CLASSICS COMPRISE *the* classics? What books *must* people read? Why should we assign these texts versus those texts? Fights over the canon are good fights, worth our time and energy. They are also risky fights with plenty of stakes, where nothing less than selfhood on the one hand and community on the other stand to be gained, or lost. How do we conduct these fights constructively?

On the face of it, the idea of a canon (in this case, a literary canon) is not particularly controversial. One can think of a canon as a stock of texts passed from one generation to the next, a way of shaping and defining a self or a community in a particular time and place. These texts can take any number of forms, from funny stories families share during reunions to books required for accreditation, such as those on a reading list used to assess graduate students during comprehensive exams. The meanings derived from these texts also vary greatly, from the punchline of a joke to a narrative identity that shapes a people. In simplest terms, a canon exists as an artifact of community and is as crucial as language and as simple as a name. Canons serve to remind a community where it has been and predict where it is going. If one derives one's identity from placing oneself in a narrative, canons supply the narratives.[20]

Much of the controversy around canons derives from the normative force they exert as a matter of course. In listing texts, canons tell a community what it should read and what stories it should tell, thereby initiating a form of life, a collective mode of saying, seeing, and acting, out of which a determinate "we" presents itself.[21] Describing a canon (*this* is what we read) prescribes a canon (this is what *we* read) and accordingly a way of being in the world (this is *how* we live).[22] We Confucians read these texts (*The Analects*; Mencius, etc.); for us this is part of what being Confucian means; reading these texts is not sufficient for being a Confucian, much less a good Confucian, but it identifies what is necessary. It would, using another example, be hard to take seriously any follower of the Black radical tradition who didn't claim the mantle of Du Bois, Baldwin, Angela Davis, or someone else in that tradition. Christianity in its turn comes not only with literary canons determined by specific regions and histories (a Latin canon in the West, a Greek canon in the East, authors and titles Evangelicals routinely consult and reference) but also an established biblical canon of sacred texts that sets the criteria of canonization itself.

While the idea of a canon is not particularly controversial, what comprises a canon almost always is. So much so that the contents of a canon should be thought of as consisting of two parts: what that canon includes and excludes, and the fights over what it includes and excludes. The fights are important to have, as necessary as they are complicated.

The fights are familiar enough: A local elementary school has to create and implement a curriculum. It cannot have the kids read everything, so it includes some things and excludes others. A fight breaks out over what it includes or excludes. The stakes are high: the youth are our future – so the worry goes – and equipping them well by inculcating them into a humanistic tradition ensures that humanity as we understand it continues. Corrupting them corrupts humanity's future.[23] Suddenly the reading list becomes all-important. If that list exclusively contains texts by white authors, it becomes hard to avoid surmising that humanness looks white. Well and good for some, but certainly not others. So much so that those whom the list renders less human begin to suspect that their exclusion is not accidental, but rather the entire point. Canon now becomes ideology, community and belonging mere ruses of power; suspicion takes over.[24]

Those fighting over what canons include and exclude recognize at a basic level the normative force exerted by a community's literary canon. This normative force sets the stakes of the fight, namely who gets to define the "we" in "we read these texts" and "this canon tells us who we should be."[25] Those claiming the current canon claim the "we" the canon describes and prescribes. Those rejecting it claim some other "we" and demand further consideration as to what counts as canon. Those refusing further consideration do so because they can, because they sit comfortably ensconced within the narrative identity the current canon describes and prescribes. It is their privilege to do so. Settled comfortably enough in their privilege, they can forget how the canon came to be, *that* the canon came to be, as an arrival of communal agreement, nothing more but also nothing less.[26]

Communities at their best keep alive the memory of how their canons became canon.[27] As soon as a community forgets that canons are made, maintained, remade, and sometimes unmade it begins to die. If it believes its canon dropped fully formed from the sky, then it has forgotten itself, forgetting that canons, like communities themselves, arrive as achievements of communal agreement, which comes through disagreement. So canon and community have diversity and difference built in.[28] A living community brims with disagreement; the absence of disagreement betokens often enough not flourishing but its opposite, decadence and the death knell of irrelevance – no one argues over texts that don't matter.[29]

Dying communities see diversity and difference as something out there, something other, them opposed to us, discontinuity to our continuity, difference over against identity, instability and chaos versus stability and order. This ploy works by projecting a mythic unity that foments a mythic disunity. Canon becomes a pawn in this game. We empty canon of its storied history, in turn emptying community of community, in order to project a false unity.[30] We do this to hide the fact that our canons get argued into existence, their histories stories of disagreement on the way to agreement. Valorizing canon – *our* unified canon as opposed to *their* disunity, instability, and chaos – has the effect of papering over all the disagreements it took to arrive at the settlement called "canon."[31] When we forget this history, invoking canon becomes a confidence game, a rhetorical pyramid scheme. Next comes the violence, ensuring adherence that communal norms on their own fail to generate. The end has begun.

If one temptation that arises in our fights over canons is entrenchment, another is giving up canon and community altogether. The controversies that erupt over community, including its canon, sometimes make people give up on community rather than fight for it. In other words, fights over canon are fights over community, and whether we any longer claim communities, and allow them to claim us. Weary and wary, we start complaining that canons are socially constructed and that their invocation is always an imposition, which paints both canon and community as oppressive.

When it comes to fights over canon, the key is to recognize the game for what it is without allowing its machinations to push us to give up canon and community altogether. Fights over the canons of Confucianism, the Black radical tradition, and Christianity are fights worth having. If it turns out that fights over their canons prove no less complex than the storied traditions themselves, that only proves the point.

Aren't the Liberal Arts Outdated?

The liberal arts remain hopelessly stuck in the past. I want to master the latest, most innovative techniques, technologies, and best practices for excelling in my profession. Reading and thinking about old ideas might be a nice hobby, but it won't help solve the complex technological problems our society faces.

Tradition Fuels Innovation

L. Gregory Jones

MORE THAN THREE DECADES AGO career government official Richard Darman derided the culture of Washington, DC, and America more broadly as preoccupied with "now-now-ism." He described it as "a shorthand label for our collective shortsightedness, our obsession with the here and now, our reluctance adequately to address the future."[1]

Darman's term insinuates not merely a reluctance to address the future but also an unwillingness to learn from the past. "Now-now-ism" results in an excessive focus on the present with little awareness of either the resources of the past or the needs of the future.

I have witnessed this tendency in church and academic cultures as well. As a result, two decades ago, I coined the term "traditioned innovation" to point to the need for ways of thinking, feeling, perceiving, and living that draw on the treasures of the past and prepare us to embrace the future with creativity and innovation.

I developed the term out of a frustration both with "now-now-ism" and with a tendency to think of innovation as "making stuff up" or creating change for the sake of change. I was struck by a conversation with Ron Heifetz, the author of *Leadership without Easy Answers*, who had popularized the term "adaptive change." He noted that most people focused on the notion of change, whereas he wanted to emphasize the importance of "adapting." His phrase had emerged from the principles of evolutionary biology: when a true transformation occurs, approximately 97 to 99 percent of the organism remains the same. The key to "adaptive change," he suggests, is knowing what to preserve as well as where to innovate.

I began to flesh out what it means to cultivate traditioned innovation as a way of life, a way of thinking and living that holds the past and future together in creative tension. As Andy Hogue and I describe it in our book *Navigating the Future: Traditioned Innovation for Wilder Seas*, traditioned innovation entails that "our feet are firmly on the ground with our hands open to the future. It requires an ongoing learning in which we are encouraged to live into the future by immersing ourselves in the best of our past, formed with a practical wisdom – what Aristotle called *phronesis* – that enables us to discern what we ought to carry forward and what we ought to leave behind."[2]

Historian Jaroslav Pelikan makes an important distinction between tradition and traditionalism: he defines tradition as "the living faith of the dead," whereas traditionalism is "the dead faith of the living."[3] Not everything from the past is worth preserving. That is why we study it: to learn what we should carry forward to enable people and the earth to flourish. Even the great works of the past and the great leaders of the past are a mix of virtue and vice, wisdom and sinfulness.

A healthy engagement with the past both cultivates the virtue of humility and enables us to have an openness to learn continually. In this life, there is much for us to discover. The liberal arts equip us to appreciate the wisdom, insights, and witness to truth, beauty, and goodness that our forebears embodied.

A healthy respect for tradition also equips us to innovate as we look to the future. That is a far cry from just "making stuff up," as so often seems to be the norm for entrepreneurship. True innovation is more like jazz improvisation or songwriting. You want to hear a jazz combo that has been steeped in tradition both by listening to past music and by learning the craft of music well – including the particularities of their instruments. What often passes for innovation today is more like the chaos of a middle-school band concert, to be endured rather than enjoyed.

Traditioned innovation is a way of nurturing the practical wisdom that Aristotle and Saint Paul and others write about: thinking, feeling, perceiving, and living in the light of those who have gone before. Our education system is too often afflicted with – and even addicted to – now-now-ism. We need to cultivate the habits and practices of traditioned innovation, along the lines Jeffrey Bilbro outlines in the following section, to equip people with the wisdom needed for transformational leadership in the twenty-first century.

The Liberating Potential of Knowing the Past

Jeffrey Bilbro

I N A N E R A of rapidly changing technologies and mores, it's entirely understandable that the past would get a bad rap: prior generations can appear atavistic, retrograde, regressive, undeveloped, and primitive. We seem to be advancing toward an almost unrecognizable future, and it's not clear how or why the past might be relevant to this new age. Nevertheless, we must not lose sight of the liberating potential of learning from the past. In brief, apprenticeship to the past liberates us in at least two ways. First, it allows us to consider where we came from. Why do we value the things we value and look at the world the way we do? If we don't examine the origins of our own assumptions and perspectives – which are largely inherited from our cultures and communities – we will never understand them and will remain thoughtlessly bound by them. Second, studying the past liberates us by providing alternatives to the blind spots of our present moment. Understanding the past – our own as well as the histories of other cultures and places – helps us imagine other possibilities for being in the world: other ways to order our economies, structure society, and relate to technologies. If we want to be free to live well as individuals and as a society, we need to engage the past as a living tradition from which we have much to learn.

Weighing Our Own Inheritance

Somewhat ironically, part of our inheritance in the West is a presentism – what C. S. Lewis calls "chronological snobbery" – that manifests as lack of interest in the past. Lewis confesses that when he was a young man he suffered from this affliction, which he defines as "the uncritical acceptance of the intellectual climate common to our own age and the assumption that whatever has gone out of date is on that account discredited." He goes on to explain how a friend taught him to remedy this condition:

> You must find why [an old idea] went out of date. Was it ever refuted (and if so by whom, where, and how conclusively) or did it merely die away as fashions do? If the latter, this tells us nothing about its truth or falsehood. From seeing this, one passes to the realization that our own age is also "a period," and certainly has, like all periods, its own characteristic illusions. They are likeliest to lurk in those widespread assumptions which are so ingrained in the age that no one dares to attack or feels it necessary to defend them.[4]

We'll return to this work of sifting through the past in order to distinguish the true from the false and to better judge our own blind spots. Here at the outset, though, we need to recognize that one feature of our contemporary culture is a reflexive disdain for the past.

The German philosopher Hans-Georg Gadamer traces this attitude to the Enlightenment era and argues that it is deeply misguided. In a wry quip he notes that "the fundamental prejudice of the Enlightenment is the prejudice against prejudice itself, which denies tradition its power." This is unfortunate because "all understanding inevitably involves some prejudice"; we make decisions, imagine possibilities, and understand reality on the basis of our inherited cultural frames of reference.[5] As Gadamer goes on to argue, "history does not belong to us; we belong to it. Long before we understand ourselves through the process of self-examination, we understand ourselves in a self-evident way in the family, society, and state in which we live. . . . *That is why the prejudices of the individual, far more than his judgments, constitute the historical reality of his being.*"[6] It can be tempting to discount this reality and imagine that our particular set of prejudices and assumptions is the default, but ignoring the ways in which we're shaped by our history doesn't free us from the shackles of the past. On the contrary, it forges these very shackles out of what should be a rich – albeit inevitably mixed – inheritance.

A better alternative to this presentist impatience with the past is to take up – deliberately and critically – the active work of tradition. Gadamer invites us to understand tradition not as some dead, static lump of events and ideas but as an inheritance that shapes us and in turn invites us to shape it. The Kentucky author Wendell Berry helpfully articulates this dynamic: "Maturity sees that the past is not to be rejected, destroyed, or replaced, but rather that it is to be judged and corrected, that the work of judgment and correction is endless, and that it necessarily involves one's *own* past."[7] This work of judgment and correction involves us in many difficulties. In his excellent book *Breaking Bread with the Dead*, Alan Jacobs wrestles with these challenges and models a way of fruitful engagement with the past. He describes this work as an active process of "taking what we have inherited and, rather than discarding it, reorganizing and reconstructing it – a task that can be performed intelligently only if we sift the past for its wisdom and its wickedness, its perception and its foolishness. And this is a task not merely for scholars but for us all."[8] We may not feel up to the challenge, but as we have all been shaped by our pasts, so we must all wrestle with this heritage if we are to be free to address contemporary problems wisely.

A caveat is in order: weighing our inheritance and actively participating in shaping our traditions is not a matter of genealogical debunking – "Oh, I now see where this value or commitment comes from and hence can see through it." Rather, it is a matter of understanding our commitments and values as tradition-informed, as rooted in a particular conversation. As Alasdair MacIntyre describes it, this posture allows us to participate in learning as a "protagonist of a particular point of view," which includes, in part, engaging in "controversy with other rival standpoints, doing so *both* in order to exhibit what is mistaken in that rival standpoint in the light of the understanding afforded by one's own point of view *and* in order to test and retest the central theses advanced from one's own point of view against the strongest possible objections to them to be derived from one's opponents."[9] Such an approach honors the reality that we are formed by our pasts. Acknowledging this allows us to participate in an ongoing shaping of tradition rather than be constrained by an unquestioned past.

Imagining Alternative Possibilities

Studying our history as active participants in a tradition frees us from an uncritical acceptance of the biases and ephemeral fads that sweep through a culture suffering from amnesia. If, as Lewis says, our age's "own characteristic illusions… are likeliest to lurk in those widespread assumptions which are so ingrained in the age that no one dares to attack or feels it necessary to defend them," then the best way to expose and judge these assumptions is by contrasting them with the views prevalent in prior eras. When we are rooted in an understanding of the past, we become aware of other possibilities for the present. With that lens, today's trends, obsessions, and assumptions no longer seem inevitable. Other possibilities exist. Being rooted in the past frees us to imagine and work toward these alternative possibilities.

It is this link between familiarity with the past and the ability to imagine alternatives to the present that leads to the paradox named in the subtitle of L. Gregory Jones's book: *traditioned innovation*. The philosopher George Santayana's inescapable adage, "Those who cannot remember the past are condemned to repeat it," follows his articulation of just this paradox: "Progress, far from consisting in change, depends on retentiveness. When change is absolute there remains no being to improve and no direction is set for possible improvement: and when experience is not retained, as among savages, infancy is perpetual."[10] Ignoring or discounting the past doesn't free us to focus on innovation and progress. Instead, it cuts us off from generations of experience and wisdom that should serve to orient our work today. Santayana's retentiveness, then, is necessary if we hope to address the roots of thorny social, cultural, or economic challenges.

Santayana's choice of words – *retentiveness* – belies the difficulty of this task. Digital media ecosystems can store vast amounts of information about the past, so we might think they would foster a healthy engagement with our cultural inheritance. But such technologies more often are used to spread viral trends on social media or to market the latest flashy gadget. In other words, such technologies tend to encourage a fixation on the concerns and priorities of the moment. And this fixation on the present renders us vulnerable to distraction. The historian Wilfred McClay extends Santayana's observation about being condemned to repeat the past and argues that "a culture without memory will be . . . easily tyrannized over. Daily events will occupy all our attention and defeat our efforts to connect past, present, and future. . . . Those who cannot remember the past are condemned to a life of aimlessness masquerading as progress."[11] "Best practices" come and go. Ephemeral trends and intellectual fads become all the rage only to be forgotten when the next cool idea goes viral.

Such is the tyranny of the all-consuming distractions on offer today.

Resisting these tendencies requires more than merely having access to a digitized library or knowing lots of facts about the past; it requires us to be deeply formed by the wisdom of the past. It should be clear by now that real innovation – wise and creative responses to new challenges – is not opposed to tradition. On the contrary, real innovation depends on people being rooted participants in a tradition. Being formed through slow conversations with past voices loads your ship's hold with the ballast necessary to keep it on course toward a worthy objective. In the same way that it is counterintuitive to load your ship with extra weight in order to speed its journey, it seems odd that we would need to study the past carefully in order to identify and pursue the right social and economic goals. Yet without that slow, patient engagement with the democracy of the dead, we'll be unable to imagine our proper end or steer a steady course, because our ship will be pushed around by the winds of today's fads.

Inheriting the Past Well

Thus far my argument for the liberating power of studying the past has remained relatively abstract. What might it look like to inherit the past well, to participate in the act of tradition? The work of judging and correcting the traditions to which we belong takes many different forms, but I'll conclude with two examples, one that is more academic and one that is more practical.

The first comes from Vincent Bacote, an African American public theologian. Bacote's work on the Dutch politician and theologian Abraham Kuyper forced him to confront the racist elements in Kuyper's work. As Bacote describes the experience, "It is no exaggeration to say that I came face to face with a figure whose words brought me delight but who then brought me to the place of decision because I had to contend with his racism. Beyond this I also had to further contend with the question of Kuyper's associations with South Africa's apartheid: Was he guilty of providing part of the theological basis for the crimes against humanity committed?" This realization led Bacote to a crisis in his endeavors to chart a coherent and contemporary public theology.

The path of least resistance for Bacote would have been simply to discard Kuyper's work and go in search of other voices, theologians who may have been less tainted by the evil of racism. But Kuyper is a seminal figure in Reformed public theology, and Bacote recognized that despite Kuyper's failings, he still had much wisdom to offer: "I chose to continue to study Kuyper's work while maintaining a critical engagement. I clearly face his failings on race (as well as his inability to transcend the intoxication of his great abilities) while appreciating and stewarding the aspects of his work that are helpful for discussions of public theology and the practice of Christian public engagement."[12] What Bacote terms "critical engagement" is precisely the work of sifting through our inheritance from the past that I have recommended in this chapter. It is the same work that Angel Adams Parham has applied herself to in building the Nyansa Classical Community. Such work is not simple or easy, but it liberates us from the failings of the past and the blind spots of the present, and it offers opportunities to discern wise approaches to pressing cultural challenges.

Bacote models a way of carefully inheriting intellectual resources from the past. In a more applied fashion, the Land Institute shows how this kind of traditioned innovation might lead to new methods of farming. The Land Institute is an agricultural research organization founded by Wes Jackson and located in Salina, Kansas. Dedicated to the pursuit of "natural systems agriculture," the Land Institute breeds plants and conducts research with the goal of developing a set of perennial polycultures that could provide food for humans. Industrial agriculture simply uproots the complex ecosystem of plants and organisms that built the rich topsoil of the American Midwest over centuries. Upon this imposed blank slate, it extracts remarkable yearly yields. Yet to achieve these yields it relies on genetically modified seeds and carefully calibrated inputs of artificial fertilizer and pesticide and herbicide. As has become apparent in recent decades, this approach uses up topsoil rather than building it, and it introduces toxins into watersheds and the broader ecosystem. The researchers at the Land Institute seek to learn from the mixed plant communities that once flourished in the Midwest and find ways to replicate that sustainable ecosystem.

Such an unorthodox approach depends on expanding the tradition within which agricultural scientists work and think. In this view, farmers can learn not only from the long history of human agriculture, which has primarily involved annual crops, but also from the mixed perennial plant communities that are more common in wild ecosystems. Aubrey Streit Krug, director of ecosphere studies at the Land Institute, writes about what it was like for her to realize the agricultural practices and assumptions she took for granted were not neutral or inevitable:

> The human newcomers who broke ground [on the prairie], eventually making the land into a "learning environment" for students like me, might have thought they were putting the past behind them. I grew up in a small wheat-farming town in nearby Kansas. The common-sense agricultural assumptions I inherited were so normal and natural to me as to be invisible. Only later did I begin to see with a shock these inherited ideas about life as a crop growing upward and forward toward a future harvest; ideas about settling fields and extracting value and digging up the roots of any problems that stand in the way.[13]

When we think we are putting the past behind us, we are in danger of destroying something we don't understand. Worse yet, we might replace it with something more destructive. Krug's work offers a better approach as she seeks to learn from the ecosystem that once thrived on the prairies and then to imagine a human agricultural system modeled on this past.

As the work of these exemplars indicates, if we want to address the root problems that result in racial injustice or ecological destruction, we can't simply condemn the past and try to develop solutions from scratch. Rather, we must engage in the patient, creative work of studying the past. This will involve both judging the errors we find there and learning from the wisdom we encounter. When we are ignorant of our pasts – our personal, communal, national, ecological, religious, or disciplinary pasts – we are not freed from their constraints or failings; we are unknowingly bound by them. Understanding this inheritance liberates us to engage it gratefully and critically. Further, it frees us from the tyranny of the present in which we are often distracted by the latest trends and obsessions. When we internalize the inheritance of the past – laying it down as ballast in our ship – we will be able to chart a steady course toward the right end.

Science as a Human Tradition

Becky L. Eggimann

IN HIS 1968 MEMOIR *The Double Helix*, James Watson shares his personal account of the discovery of the structure of DNA.[14] This discovery, which allowed scientists to understand DNA's self-replication mechanism and launched the modern biochemical era, is one of the greatest scientific discoveries of all time. But what is even more relevant to me, as a chemist with appreciation for liberal arts learning, is the way Dr. Watson's story unfolds. He takes "personal" seriously, sharing his thoughts and feelings at each step of the journey. He also uses effective storytelling to draw the reader into the world of scientific practice. We see how this bit of science was really done, including the overt and unexamined sexism and competitiveness that were part of science in this time and place.

What we learn from Watson is that scientific discoveries are far from inevitable. Working out the DNA double helix took a lot of energy, expert knowledge, trial-and-error guesswork, political maneuvering, countless conversations with scientists around the world, and good old-fashioned luck. This discovery, like all scientific discoveries, was built on a vast tradition of investigative know-how and craftsmanship. In one memorable moment, Watson and fellow scientist Francis Crick were stuck trying to understand how the nitrogen-rich bases fit into the interior of the helix. They were relying on published versions of the structures for each base, but the structures didn't line up properly for the necessary hydrogen bonds. After a conversation with another scientist, a structural chemist who had studied similar small organic molecules, Watson and Crick learned that the textbook structures were almost certainly wrong. Scientists with structural know-how were using a different version, a tautomeric form known to be more prevalent in experimental observations. Switching to the alternate tautomer led Watson and Crick to quickly identify the A-T and G-C base-pairing rules we know today and accelerated their understanding of the double-helix structure.

I enjoy reading *The Double Helix* with my students because it reads like an adventure story, with a brash hero and a world-altering final outcome. Students get caught up in the excitement of discovery. With a bit of prodding, they also begin to see that there is a tradition and culture at work, which shaped the *way* this scientific discovery was made and *who* was able to make it.

When I began conducting research full-time as part of my PhD, I joined a research lab and entered an apprenticeship to understand a particular method: molecular simulation. I was immersed in this technique and the traditions and culture that surround it, learning not just how to do it, but its unique artistry. I learned what simulation was good for and how it advanced knowledge for the good of society. I also learned its limitations, and how to keep it within the boundaries of its effectiveness. I was taught to read the literature in a certain way. Most practitioners, I was taught, fail to appreciate the complexity and scope of the method, making mistakes that reduced its accuracy or efficiency. Some groups were trustworthy, having proven themselves through high-quality work, and we read all their papers. Other groups (and their papers) could be ignored. I joined a community of practice, absorbing its traditions and values through the culture of the lab. Only when I began to see my simulations as a craft, requiring artistry and a connection to past tradition, did I begin to make contributions that others found meaningful.

In our attempts to make science accessible, we often present past discoveries as obvious and ready-made. They seem to be inevitable, immutable truths, devoid of history, that transcend context and culture. Public perception about the power of science to solve the world's problems draws upon this naive understanding. Many of us, often without realizing it or meaning to, reduce the thorny problems of society to merely technical ones. For example, coronavirus vaccines were promised as the silver-bullet solution to the pandemic, yet cultural factors like equitable distribution and the spread of misinformation left that promise only partially fulfilled. Simplistic views of science miss, or at least gloss over, the human tradition, history, and culture of scientific discovery. We want to ignore or simply forget that science is a practiced craft, shaped and fashioned according to shared traditions and community values, all things that can and should be examined and sometimes reformed, for example by expanding these communities to welcome women and people of color.

We understand science best when we understand it as a human tradition with its own histories and cultures, much as Dr. Watson shows us in *The Double Helix*. One of my colleagues has gained a reputation as a particularly effective teacher because he introduces quantum mechanics through the lens of the initial experiments that generated unexplained anomalies in the early twentieth century. He invites students to imagine why these results were so befuddling and exciting in their time and context. He relays science as a story, following the history of the discoveries and controversies until the climactic conclusion where quantized energies explain all the anomalies. Students remember this, even to the point of telling me about it years later. When I began graduate school, I encountered something similar. In my first course on molecular simulation, the instructor introduced the topic not using a textbook but through the original papers that established the field. We walked through the first simulation ever published, learning what was unique and groundbreaking, and we kept walking through each of the subsequent breakthroughs until we had a deep appreciation for the history and maturity of the methods we were using.

We all know from experience that science (and technologies derived from science) can be powerful forces for the benefit of society. A closer look at the practice of science helps us appreciate that each breakthrough emerges within and because of a human tradition with a history and culture. Discoveries are largely recognized – and at times constructed – through cycles of community engagement with data and methods, informed by traditions and values.

Eventually, the community refines its understanding until there is consistency of interpretation, replicability, and accurate predictions of future data. In this way, science depends on its past, and we become better scientists when we value, learn, and examine its histories and traditions.

Aren't the Liberal Arts
Out of Touch?

Maybe you ivory tower academics haven't
noticed, but the world is busted. I want to do
something about it. I want to make an impact.
Right now. How is reading old books going
to help me feed the hungry and liberate the
oppressed and reverse climate change?

Art Matters

Steve Prince

HENRIK IBSEN ALLEGEDLY SAID, "A thousand words leave not the same deep impression as does a single deed." Over time his words have been paraphrased and immortalized as "a picture is worth a thousand words." When I think of Ibsen's quote, the word "epistle" comes to mind. The apostle Paul writes, "You are our epistle written in our hearts, . . . written not with ink but by the Spirit of the living God, not on tablets of stone but on tablets of flesh, that is, of the heart."[1] Our bodies are a living letter, an epistle. What we create, read, learn, decipher, understand, remember, and pass on through our incarnated lives is essential to unlocking the mysteries of the past to create a more just and equitable future. Countless individuals, sung and unsung, have stood in the tide of indifference girded with a clear understanding of what is just and true. History has shown us that the arts are germane to our survival. Seeing the world through the lens of the arts, whether it be poetry, music, dance, or visual arts, deconstructs the world into a series of questions.

Each question peels back another layer of our perception, pushing us to imagine a little deeper. Martin Luther King Jr. told the world "I have a dream." Malcolm X said that we must survive "by any means necessary." Marvin Gaye asked, "What's going on?" Sam Cooke said, "A change is gonna come." Billie Holiday told us "southern trees bear a strange fruit." Maya Angelou let us know "why the caged bird sings." Alvin Ailey's blood memories of growing up in the Black church in the south are manifested in "Revelations." Nikki Giovanni told us that "Black love is Black wealth." Sojourner Truth asked, "Ain't I a woman?" Tupac Shakur encouraged his community to "keep your head up," while Curtis Mayfield eloquently urged us all to "keep on pushing."

Steve Prince, *Rosa Sparks*, linoleum cut on paper

There's far more to any work of art than meets the eye at first. Let me give you an example. Prior to the Covid pandemic I created a linoleum cut titled *Rosa Sparks*. The image commemorates Rosa Parks, who refused to give up her seat and was subsequently arrested for civil disobedience on a Montgomery, Alabama, bus in December 1955. Parks's bravery was the "spark" for the Montgomery bus boycott. My image encapsulates the pivotal moment when the bus driver tried to get Parks to surrender her seat to a white passenger. In his Epistle to the Ephesians, Paul says we must put on "the whole armor of God," because we battle not against flesh and blood but against principalities and things in high places. Parks is clad in this armor: the breastplate of righteousness, the shield of faith, the helmet of salvation.[2] Her posture is in opposition to the driver, and she says with her body, "I will not be moved."

You don't need to be a psychologist to decipher her defiance from her stance and her cold glare. Following Parks's arrest, masses of Black people mobilized under the leadership of Martin Luther King Jr., picketing, carpooling, walking, and riding bikes for over a year, causing the local government to relent and integrate the buses. The people collectively affected the local economy and awakened the nation to the power of the collective spirit. At the top of my composition men and women walk in a tessellation field of black and white, symbolizing the protest penetrating the unequal busing system. The people carry signs that say, "I AM," which alludes to the "I Am a Man" signs wielded by sanitation workers in Memphis, Tennessee, when King came to their aid shortly before he was slain by an assassin's bullet. I removed the "A Man" portion to reference what God said to Moses when Moses asked, "What shall I call you when I go before Pharaoh?" God said, "Tell him I AM has sent me to you."[3] I believe the divine protected people during the civil rights era, so they could endure and evoke change in stultifying systems.

We may have some victories under our belt from the sacrifices of people who put their lives and livelihoods on the line for change, but we still have several issues in the back of the conceptual "bus" to grapple with. In the shadows of this print the letters "ET" are conspicuously attached to the hat of a ghost-like figure, which represents Emmett Till, a fourteen-year-old boy who was murdered in Mississippi earlier in 1955 for supposed "reckless eyeballing." Till had traveled from Chicago to spend time with his cousins. On the third day after he was murdered, his body was pulled from the bottom of the Tallahatchie River, beaten beyond recognition. When his body arrived in Chicago and his mother went to the morgue to identify her son, she smelled the stench of his body two blocks away. Her next gesture, using his body as an epistle for the whole world to read, could not be contained in any book, or poem, or song, or artwork; we were confronted with the raw nature of our existence and the question: What is America doing to its children? An "X" for Malcolm, and a "crown" for King allude to the two leaders who were assassinated in 1965 and 1968, respectively, fighting for the cause. A Black man with his hands upraised represents Michael Brown, killed by police in Ferguson, Missouri. Next to him a young Black male with a hoodie and a can of Arizona iced tea represents Trayvon Martin, who was slain in Sanford, Florida, in 2012. He stands in for Eric Garner, who uttered "I can't breathe!" while being choked by a police officer in New York City in 2014. Ironically, these are the same words George Floyd said in 2020 in Minneapolis, Minnesota, before his death under the knee of a police officer. A mother and child peacefully sit amid the hate-storm. The two are sacred figures. I removed the halos that would traditionally adorn the heads of Mary and Christ. I wanted to create figures that represent the deity that I believe we all represent every day. Each one of our lives, regardless of race, ethnicity, or class, is sacred and beautiful. The woman holds a Bible open to the words, "Blessed are the peacemakers, for they shall be called children of God."[4]

During the summer of 2020, at the height of racial unrest in America, I was struck with a great sense of weariness because I had heard this song before and I was tired of its tune. After a conversation with my brother, he encouraged me by saying, "This is the time that you have been working for, no time to sit and sulk." I was reminded of Galatians 6:9: "Let us not grow weary of doing good, for in due season we will reap, if we do not give up." We must continue the march, we must continue to create, we must continue to imagine, we must continue to challenge damaging constructions, we must commit and submit our art to truth, and we must use the power of imagination to be the living epistles we were created to be.

A Richer Sense of Relevance

Noah Toly

ARE THE LIBERAL ARTS RELEVANT? While some recoil at the question, I think it's a good one. My current and past employers, both of which have played a role in the project that resulted in this book, have been Christian liberal arts institutions. While the two are different in important ways, they have much in common, and neither seems content to concede the irrelevance of a liberal arts education. In fact, relevance is right there in the mission statement of each school:

> Wheaton College serves Jesus Christ and advances His Kingdom through excellence in liberal arts and graduate programs that educate the whole person to build the church and benefit society worldwide.[5]

> Calvin University equips students to think deeply, to act justly, and to live wholeheartedly as Christ's agents of renewal in the world.[6]

With ambitious mission statements like these, we shouldn't be surprised when students show up looking for an education that's relevant. We should expect them to come wondering whether the education they'll get will help them understand and address topics ranging from mass incarceration, climate change, war, and poverty to artificial intelligence, urban infrastructure, and energy breakthroughs. We've promised to help them respond wisely and redemptively to events in the headlines, from pandemics to protests.

Those promises aren't a new twist. They're not a desperate response to the market, a concession to the zeitgeist, or a bait-and-switch plot to enroll students interested in relevance, only to convince them later that relevance doesn't matter. No, those promises are part of our DNA. The liberal arts have *always* promised relevance.[7]

So champions of liberal arts education don't need to correct those who want relevance, because a liberal arts education has always been about relevance, and they don't need to sell students on relevance, because students already want it. But they *do* need to show how liberal arts distinctively delivers on the promise of relevance. Not merely that a liberal arts education teaches skills, like reading and writing, that are useful in many occupations, nor that it prepares students for a career in which they might change jobs eighteen times. It's true that liberal arts education is applicable in these ways, and that's a good thing. But if vocational open-endedness is the most that advocates can claim for the relevance of a liberal arts education, then it might be a lost cause.

The good news is there's so much more to say: A liberal arts education awakens students to a deeper, richer sense of relevance. It invites them to reappraise what counts as relevant, opening them up to surprising insights and unanticipated connections and helping them see that relevance is not only about what we know but about who we are.

One distinctive mark of a liberal arts education is its scope of study. On the one hand, the liberal arts cannot be defined by the breadth of the curriculum (though some are inclined to characterize them this way). On the other hand, it is inconceivable that a liberal arts education would be limited to an exclusive focus on any area of study. Whether we're talking about the trivium and quadrivium or a canon of modern disciplines descended from or expanding on those paths of study, the liberal arts help us understand an array of subjects and ways of knowing. The point of this scope isn't merely to understand discrete fields, but to understand how they relate to each other. For example, it's not just to understand the humanities *and* the sciences; it's to understand the humanities *in relation to* the sciences. A liberal arts education helps us grasp an ecosystem of understanding – an ecosystem that is more responsive to the challenges we see in the world than is any one discipline. From artificial intelligence to urban infrastructure, from climate change to conflict, one of the characteristics of so-called "real-world" challenges is that they defy disciplinary and professional boundaries. Nothing could be more relevant than understanding connections between fields of study. By providing a foundation in these connections, a liberal arts education helps us to respond appropriately to the challenges of our time. As environmental historian William Cronon writes, "More than anything else, being an educated person means being able to see connections that allow one to make sense of the world and act within it in creative ways. . . . A liberal education is about gaining the power and the wisdom, the generosity and the freedom to connect."[8]

Just as it helps us see the connections between areas of study, a liberal arts education also helps us understand that, regardless of the challenges and opportunities before us, addressing them does not require us to make our own beginning. A liberal arts education draws from deep wells of wisdom that apply to everything from headline news to the greatest issues of our time. A student interested in social media may assume the relevance of a business course on marketing, but may be pleasantly surprised to learn that Aristotle's reflections on friendship or Tocqueville's on civic associations are relevant to the same topic. The principle extends to nearly every challenge we might consider: there is no struggle for emancipation that cannot be informed by thousands of years of thought about the meaning of freedom, no effort at sustainability and conservation that cannot be informed by the long history of wrestling with our limits, no opportunity to make and do that cannot be shaped by better understanding the consequences of our inventions. Liberal education teaches us where to find these wells and how to drink deeply from them. It brings timeless resources into conversation with timely challenges. It isn't relevant *and* resourceful, it's relevant *because* it's resourceful.

Liberal education prizes inquiry. Whether apart from or paired with a professional education, the liberal arts prepare us with a mindset, toolset, and soulset for framing questions and a wariness of beginning with the answers in mind. This isn't important because questions are somehow more relevant than answers – they're not – but because questions, especially good ones, lead to relevant answers. In fact, when we think we know the answers before we even set out the questions, that's when we risk doing work of the greatest irrelevance. That's when we risk finding ourselves, as the French social theorist Jacques Ellul notes, "in the presence of a large number of solutions . . . that do not respond to any problem posed – or more precisely the problem is posed well enough in the reality, in the practical life, but it is not formulated." "It is impossible," Ellul continues, "to answer a question when the question is not thus posed."[9] A liberal education teaches students the disposition, skill, and humility to discover good questions – questions in service of more relevant answers.[10]

Finally, a liberal arts education is relevant because, at its best, it is not only informative, but also formative. It doesn't just fill our heads with knowledge but shapes our whole person. Some refer to this as well-roundedness. But the point of well-roundedness isn't to know a little about a lot of things; it's to be shaped by our encounters with each other in a shared engagement with the treasures that are the humanities, arts, and natural and social sciences, regardless of the vocations to which we might finally connect them. Authentic communities devoted to inquiry, informed by the resources of the centuries, and aware of the ecosystem of knowledge shape curious and courageous people. Liberal education isn't the *only* way we can become that kind of people – there are other types of institutions and practices that can result in similar formation – nor does it have uniform effects. But it prepares us to be the kind of people who address the challenges and opportunities of the moment, people with the daring and disciplined imaginations needed to fulfill the most ambitious – and relevant – missions.

Stories and Severed Selves

Erin Shaw

WE ARE COLLECTORS OF STORIES, and the stories we collect make us the people we are. My work as an artist rests in this simple assertion. I am a citizen of the Chickasaw nation and of Choctaw descent, and an artist and a professor of visual arts at John Brown University.

In narrative style, I create paintings engaged in story: both its function and its telling. I see my role in this process as mediator and disrupter: standing between two oppositions, separating them, placing boundaries in new and unusual places and joining them once again. I work in this manner that I might see things in a new way. As an artist, I am profoundly interested and invested in stories and their power. As much as the paint and canvas, my medium is stories.

Years ago, I created a body of work called *Claim the Sky*.[11] It's a story about a bird in a cage, singing the words it is told to sing. The bird finds its release and sings its song. In the process of making *Claim the Sky*, I painted myself out of that cage. I sincerely believe this.

As a Native American woman, I am surrounded and known by my ancestors, who teach me about place, stewardship, community, mutuality in relationships, integration, and love of creation. Yet I live in a world ruled by power, greed, time, hierarchy, and utility, and split into fragments. I have a foot in both worlds. I feel and know this tension intimately. For many years, I wavered between embracing either my Native American heritage or my European worldview. I could not see a way for both to coexist. In those years, I lived in a duality causing me to fragment. In that fragmentation, I found a truncated, divided, and shallow existence.

But this particular tension has also created opportunities for me. Because of the tension I experience, my cultural identity provides a necessary path toward human integration outside of a dominant Western construct. It compels me to look for connection where others see separation. This is one of the great disciplines of my life. In the classroom with young artists and students, I bring my work of integration: How can we develop whole, integrated, thriving humans who understand how to ask good questions, how to use their creativity to bless the world, who resist the need to create more separations and can flourish in all contexts because they themselves are flourishing as human beings?

Too often fragmentation dominates the American story. We divide and dehumanize one another. Echoing repeatedly is a refrain of division and separation. Within universities, companies, friendships, and even families, the story of rupture is loud and unsettling. How are today's students to respond to the cultural fracturing they've inherited? Will they know how to flourish in a time defined by polarized beliefs?

If we are to heal our large cultural fractures, we need to first heal our individual fractures. To become fully integrated human beings, we must intentionally, deliberately create a space for personal cultural renewal.

In my advanced drawing class, I ask students to create from an integrated base. Students look intentionally at their intellects: What ideas are they carrying around? What are they curious about? What are they reading, seeing, hearing? What concepts do they have about these things? If there is a place where their spiritual life and emotional life seem in opposition, how can they create a connection? And finally, I ask them to integrate their bodies with the work as well. This can include technique or how they are using materials. By pressing the students to think about these things individually and bring them all to the work they are doing, a strong sense of integration arises.

One student talked about how much sleep he missed during that course, but that it was like nothing he had ever done before and that he would miss sleep any day for the experience. It was healing for him and made him feel like he began to find his voice.

In this same course, I had a student who had suffered tremendous emotional and physical abuse as a child. When I began asking students to push into their emotions as well, she was initially very angry. But she quickly saw that she had marginalized a large part of who she was, and as she moved through the course of the semester, incredible emotional healing came. If you knew her before and after, you would agree that she is a totally different person. Walking toward personal integration through her course work as an artist is literally changing her.

Working in higher education, I have found that there are many people who want to quantify an education in studio art via some perceived career. When we commodify art in these terms, we strip much of its implicit power. Many of my students talk about how doing what they love is a way for them to combat the drudgery of life. They seem to understand they could have more financially driven goals, but they would be sacrificing some level of passion and engagement as well as the opportunity to impact people, history, and culture.

This type of education, educating the different aspects of a student with the goal of integrating them into a whole person, is not just relevant but necessary. I could say that much is at stake, but the truth is that everything is at stake. Our cultural fragmentation is a direct result of individual fragmentation. If you ask students to make connections, ask good questions, and think broadly within their studies, they begin to understand how to do that work within themselves and on larger scales as well. We must create a space for integration. The liberal arts do just that. If we want to heal the deeper divides in our society, we need to first heal our severed selves.

Aren't Liberal Arts Degrees Unmarketable?

Thinking deeply and contributing to social change sound great, but at the end of the day I really just want to get a good job and enjoy a comfortable standard of living. I can't afford to spend four years and accrue thousands of dollars of debt if I don't end up with marketable skills. People who study the liberal arts end up as baristas.

Why Engineers Need the Liberal Arts

David Hsu

"WHY SHOULD ENGINEERS CARE about the liberal arts?" I know high school students ponder some version of this question as they consider the vast array of college options before them. After all, students can attend a four-year engineering program at a university and take a primarily technical course load. This appears more practical than attending a liberal arts college that requires a broad range of classes in the humanities and social sciences that engineers often hope to avoid. Engineers are predisposed positivists – they find truth in the scientific method and the laws of physics, not in learning to read Tolstoy or interpreting Edvard Munch. The common belief is that companies desire engineering graduates who have had the most technically rigorous training, so why spend time studying philosophy and art history at a liberal arts college?

A 2019 survey conducted by the University Professional and Continuing Education Association confirms that graduates with technical training in STEM (science, technology, engineering, and math) disciplines have a better job outlook than liberal arts majors. The survey found that STEM majors were employed at a higher rate (73 percent full-time) than liberal arts majors (55 percent full-time).[1] Furthermore, STEM majors rated their overall satisfaction with their salary more highly than liberal arts majors. So, if a STEM major is associated with greater employability and higher salaries, then from a pragmatic standpoint, why bother with the liberal arts at all? Josh Dortzbach tells a different story.

During his visit to one of my engineering classes, Josh, who earned dual degrees in engineering and liberal arts, presented on the projects his structural engineering firm had worked on in the past decade. Along with exquisite hotels and residential high-rises in downtown Chicago, his projects included redeveloping a hundred-year-old building once used for meat packing into a modern commercial office space now occupied by Google. His firm had also provided the structural framing plan for a Willow Creek Church worship facility designed by Adrian Smith, the architect behind the world's tallest building, the Burj Khalifa. Josh's successes drew from a much broader background than a technical degree could provide. Over a decade ago, Josh decided to start his own firm. As he described his career, it became clear that no amount of technical training alone could have prepared him for the task of establishing a structural engineering consulting business. This required crafting a meaningful business mission and philosophy, communicating well with global clients, developing a culture of collaboration within a diverse team, navigating complex ethical dilemmas, solving multifaceted sociotechnical problems, and ensuring that the firm's solutions were "guided by the context of history and experience." Josh concluded by stating, "My engineering degree may have gotten me a job, but my liberal arts degree makes me good at my job."

Indeed, engineers need the liberal arts to be effective. It is a myth that engineers can draw a black box around the technical aspects of their work and expect the social outcomes to be fruitful for affected communities. Rather, the social aspects must always be considered alongside the technical to dependably effect human flourishing. To do this well requires a liberal arts foundation and approach. Steve Jobs revealed one of the secrets to Apple's success after introducing the iPad 2 in 2011: "Technology alone is not enough – it's technology married with liberal arts, married with the humanities, that yields us the result that makes our heart sing."[2]

Engineers also need the liberal arts to be marketable. A survey conducted by the National Association of Colleges and Employers in 2018 found that the most employable skills were communication, problem-solving, and collaboration.[3] A survey administered in four Asian countries found that those same skills were among the most sought after in engineering hires – skills that are honed in the liberal arts tradition.[4] Even within engineering design, the most vital mindsets are empathy, human-centeredness, and critical thinking. Don Weinkauf, dean of the School of Engineering at the University of St. Thomas, asks his students, "What type of experience do you think would prepare you to thrive in an environment where there are a thousand possible answers to every question: your math class or your philosophy class?"[5]

Engineers also need the liberal arts to stay relevant. The National Academy of Engineers 2004 strategic report stated, "The comfortable notion that a person learns all that he or she needs to know in a four-year engineering program just is not true and never was. Not even the 'fundamentals' are fixed, as new technologies enter the engineer's toolkit. Engineers are going to have to accept responsibility for their own continual reeducation, and engineering schools are going to have to prepare engineers to do so by teaching them how to learn." [6] The ability to learn and adapt fostered by the liberal arts is precisely why the rate of salary growth for some liberal arts majors exceeds that of engineering graduates. Although engineering and computer science majors begin their careers making 37 percent more than history and social science majors, that gap closes by age forty. [7] Engineers may find that the skills they gained in the academy lose applicability quickly in an environment where technology is rapidly evolving, whereas interpersonal skills, communication, and adaptability never fade in relevance.

So, why should engineers care about the liberal arts? One might respond: Can an engineer afford to live without them? Engineers today must have greater social awareness for effective design; they must possess strong collaborative proclivity, problem-solving capability, and interpersonal competence; and they must demonstrate relentless adaptability to rapid technological and cultural shifts. Engineers who neglect the liberal arts will struggle to meet these challenges.

Forming Better Professionals and Leaders

Rachel B. Griffis

I N MANY INSTITUTIONS of higher education, there is an uneasy relationship between the professional programs and the humanities or liberal arts departments. Students majoring in a professional degree track may feel that classes outside their major are a waste of time, and students may be reluctant to major in a discipline traditionally associated with the liberal arts. Such tensions are unfortunate because they ignore the reality that a liberal arts formation prepares students not only to use their skills and knowledge to thrive personally and benefit their broader communities but also to succeed in an unpredictable economy. Professional training and liberal arts formation are not in competition; they are complementary. Indeed, some schools have found ways to ease these felt tensions and provide students with professional training in a liberal arts context. Such institutions can provide a model for offering students the credentials they perceive as valuable while embedding this training in a more robust educational vision.

False Dichotomies between Liberal Arts and Earning Potential

One of the unfortunate results of the tension between professional programs and traditional liberal arts classes is that study in the latter realm is assumed to be unprofitable. Defenders of the liberal arts don't help their case when their arguments for the preservation of the liberal arts exclusively emphasize the intangible goods of this approach to education while downplaying, or even vilifying, students' concerns about financial security. Many advocates of liberal arts majors try to convince students of the superiority of their field through the suggestion that monetary motivation for study is shallow or inferior. For example, Mark Edmundson champions the English major because it is "pursuing the most important subject of all – being a human being."[8] In *Education's End*, Anthony T. Kronman narrates his journey through an undergraduate philosophy course, a morally and intellectually stimulating experience that serves to illustrate his point that higher education should provide students with goods beyond earning potential. He writes, "At the heart of the seminar was the question of how best to live, of what to care about and why, the question of the meaning of life."[9] In a manner that veers into chastising students who are only interested in the monetary value of a college degree, and the institutions that cater to them, Wes Jackson laments, "The universities now offer only one serious major: upward mobility."[10] Writing specifically to students enrolled at Christian liberal arts colleges, Jeffry C. Davis employs a religious argument to warn students against prioritizing money in their studies by citing Jesus, who insisted, "You cannot serve God and money."[11]

Although such arguments indeed convey an important claim – that earning potential is not the only point of education and that it should not be a student's sole priority – the writers and educators I've referenced (and others) nevertheless communicate an unwelcome, often implicit, message to students and parents regarding the liberal arts: they are not profitable. By setting up a false dichotomy between gainful employment and the humanizing goods of the liberal arts, we are unwittingly dismissing legitimate questions from students regarding their ability to flourish with a liberal arts education. As Andrew Delbanco points out, "This is not a question of either/or"; students in professional programs should "have their minds stretched by the big questions raised by history, science, philosophy, and the arts," and "by the same token, students in traditional liberal arts fields need to gain the concrete skills that are required in a demanding labor market."[12] Preservation of the liberal arts in our educational institutions, therefore, depends on us rejecting the false dichotomy between professional training and a liberal arts education and championing the profitability of the liberal arts and the ways in which this approach to education prepares students to thrive financially. After all, it's hard to contemplate the meaning of life or invest in the well-being of your community if you're worried about where the next rent check will come from.

Evidence for the Profitability of the Liberal Arts

Richard A. Detweiler's study *The Evidence Liberal Arts Needs: Lives of Consequence, Inquiry, and Accomplishment* (2021) provides empirical data suggesting that the liberal arts not only cultivate graduates devoted to the common good and a purposeful existence but indeed also prepare students to reach higher incomes over the course of their careers as well as to advance to more prestigious positions within their fields.[13] In his analysis of the mission statements of selected liberal arts institutions in the United States, Detweiler identifies "living a personally successful life" as one of the goals of a liberal arts education, along with "altruism," "leadership," and "cultural involvement." Rather than dismiss or discount "living a personally successful life," which he measures by annual income and level of professional position, as a shallow or inferior motivation for a college degree, Detweiler counts it as legitimate and among several other outcomes of the liberal arts, even if this outcome is "less directly related to long-held liberal arts purposes." In doing so, he acknowledges ways in which the institutional forms that the liberal arts take in twenty-first-century America differ from those in ancient Greece, taking in stride one of the most pressing questions both students and parents have about the value of higher education.

Detweiler's study shows a statistically significant connection between higher income levels over the long-term and individuals who received a liberal arts education. He notes that "while first job placement and income may be better for those with specialized training, this advantage disappears rather quickly." Rather than measuring only a graduate's potential to land a high-paying position immediately after obtaining a degree, Detweiler takes stock of liberal arts graduates thirty and forty years post-college. In particular, he found that "those who studied more broadly by taking more than half of their courses outside their major were 24 percent more likely to report a higher income as adults." Moreover, this finding has implications for diversity, equity, and inclusion work, as the gap "was more substantial" among students of lower socioeconomic status. Detweiler's conclusion is worth quoting at length, as it provides a compelling answer to our question regarding the profitability of the liberal arts. He writes:

> The idea that there is no substantial relationship between having a vocation-oriented major and longer-term success is interesting, given that people, ranging from students and parents to policymakers, have become increasingly concerned that college should result in a good job. Yet specialized study is not the predictor of longer-term success; our research findings emphasize the importance of breadth of study for all, especially those who enter college from less economically advantaged families.

Narratives from Detweiler's study enrich his statistical findings and provide further explanation for the profitability of a broad, rather than specialized, education. He includes the story of a journalism major, Alison, who spent significant time during college studying and practicing music, which she insists, "worked to teach the whole person, not just the journalist I would become." She explains, "I learned how to balance the work I needed to do for my classes with my rehearsal schedule. . . . I am now employed full time as a reporter for a newspaper, and every day I use the skills my four years . . . taught me." Another graduate with a liberal arts education, Bill, draws attention to the ways he has benefitted from his various avenues of collegiate study over his forty-year career as a broadcast executive. He says, "I received a broad, liberal arts exposure to several disciplines that fed my natural curiosity," which provided "setup for success in my career. . . . What was important to me then, and continues to be now, was the ability to explore widely and to absorb things that were of little use until later in my career – when they suddenly were." These narratives help explain why a professional program or vocational major, such as nursing or engineering, may help a student get a good first job, but over the long term, students such as Alison and Bill continue using their broad knowledge to advance in their fields and to recognize profitable opportunities when they arise.

Given that Detweiler's study identifies a specific connection between taking more than half one's courses outside one's major and annual income and professional position, his book also makes the striking argument that "college major is unrelated to longer-term success." Rather, "greater success over the longer term accrues to those who study more broadly and are more involved with faculty and mentors outside of class." Again, the narratives he includes from liberal arts graduates indicate why. Deborah, an interdisciplinary studies major who focused on sociology, Spanish, and Latin American studies, worked her way up to a senior-level position at a major corporation. She confronts the popular opinion that an individual with her education is not prepared for the kind of success she now enjoys by insisting, "My liberal arts education did not prepare me for one particular job or profession; it prepared me for any that I would choose." She goes on to explain "three critical things that have made all the difference: How to Learn, How to Think, and How to Communicate," which she describes as "the broad-based perspective and agility that support problem-solving and characterize any successful career, with all its twists and turns, its challenges and opportunities." Deborah's testimony regarding the value of her interdisciplinary major is affirmed by a *New York Times* opinion piece in which Frank Bruni asserts, "Regardless of major, there are skills to insist on acquiring because they transcend any particular career." The skills he recommends acquiring are "communication and storytelling." He tells students, "Take a course in Greek mythology, British literature, political rhetoric, or anything else that exposes you to the structure of narrative and the art of persuasion."[14] What becomes clear through both Bruni's advice to college students and Detweiler's study is that the profitability of the liberal arts hinges on their nonspecialized nature. Formation in the basic human arts of communication, persuasion, and narration proves to be essential to success in almost any career path.

Implications

The liberal arts are indeed profitable, and students who are concerned with getting a good job and not becoming baristas after college should be encouraged to invest in this style of education. Moreover, proponents of the liberal arts would do well to emphasize their profitability, alongside the other goods they offer, taking care not to dismiss the student who aspires to make a comfortable living. Although greed is certainly a feature of contemporary life, financial security is an aspect of human flourishing that should not be villainized, especially to students who have seen or experienced suffering as a result of business shutdowns, layoffs, and economically turbulent times.

One significant barrier that students and educators seem to face regarding the question of the profitability of the liberal arts is what Wheaton provost Karen An-hwei Lee refers to as parents' and students' desire for a "clear one-to-one connection" between "the name of a major" and a particular job.[15] Lee describes a liberal arts major as offering "multilinear pathways" into the workforce, a prospect that tends not to appeal to students and parents. Instead, these "multilinear pathways" appear risky when compared to the safety of majoring in a field such as nursing, which promises to produce a nurse with a paycheck. Educators, consequently, may need to take up the task of helping students and parents to see the limits of preparing solely for a particular first job after college. Detweiler's research indicates how long-term career planning is likely to provide a return on investment. As students prepare for a lifetime of professional success, they will need knowledge and skills to help them with tasks and jobs that do not currently exist and in situations they cannot yet imagine. For example, Rosemary Barnes, who graduated in 2005 with majors in both engineering and philosophy, noted in an opinion piece in 2020 that the skills she learned in her engineering major that were meant to prepare her for a job "were laughably out of date within five years of graduation."[16] She explains, "Important fields that I have become an expert in now did not exist when I was at university." On the other hand, her studies in philosophy continue to serve as a foundation for her success as an engineer. She writes, "The main skills you learn in a humanities degree are timeless," and they "have made me a far better engineer than I would have been without them."

A final consideration regarding the profitability of the liberal arts is to explore how Detweiler defines this approach to education and to recognize ways it can be incorporated into professional programs. Comparing American college or university education to institutions of higher learning around the world, Detweiler notes that liberal arts approaches are indeed something of a tradition in the United States and that most institutions contain vestiges of them in their curricula. Detweiler identifies "attributes of education in the tradition of the liberal arts," some of which are related to breadth of content, though others illuminate the "educational context," which includes "engaging pedagogy" and "authentic learning community." Where educators in professional programs may be unable to require the breadth of study that students get in more traditional programs, they can still strive to use engaging pedagogies and cultivate authentic learning communities, thus providing students with opportunities not only to learn deeply but to benefit from the long-term goods such relational formation provides.

Further, institutions with values-oriented missions that focus on offering professional programs can incorporate the breadth of study that is associated with the liberal arts into what would be a very narrow course of study elsewhere. For example, Dordt University, a Reformed Christian institution, began a two-year "Pro-Tech" program in 2017 that offers associate degrees in farm operations and manufacturing. This program aspires "to go further than most vocational schools, providing students with a holistic Christian education that will prepare them for every aspect of their lives."[17] In addition to taking specialized courses such as "Farm Safety and Equipment," students also take classes aimed at their holistic development: "Kingdom, Identity, and Calling," "Biblical Foundations," and "Leading and Serving Others." As Detweiler's study affirms, "nonvocational" coursework is integral to the many positive outcomes of a liberal arts education, including financial success, which bodes well for professional programs such as those at Dordt University that go beyond technical training.

Dordt's Pro-Tech program resonates with Detweiler's identification of "authentic community" as integral to the liberal arts because students enrolled in the Pro-Tech program live on campus, attend chapel, and function as members of the student body alongside those seeking four-year degrees. In an interview with *The Liberating Arts* podcast, Dordt's president, Erik Hoekstra, describes Pro-Tech students' participation in the wider community as "liberating," referencing ways that life on campus encourages these students to acquire a breadth of experiences during their studies.[18] In particular, he commends Pro-Tech students who join the orchestra and sing in the choir, suggesting that these nonvocational activities are a significant part of a student's education. Finally, Hoekstra also gestures toward the ways in which these professional programs contribute to social and economic justice by dismantling "hierarchies" or "caste systems" in American society, in which people with "white collars" tend to be more important than those who make their living through manual labor. Both the content of the Pro-Tech program, which aims to educate the whole person in addition to teaching technical skills, and the context, which welcomes these students into the life of the community, function, in Hoekstra's words, to "liberate the frontline worker." Although Dordt's Pro-Tech program is undoubtedly different from other liberal arts institutions discussed in this book, it nevertheless incorporates aspects of the liberal arts that are linked to both intrinsic and professional benefits of this approach to education, and it deserves recognition and consideration in conversations about the preservation and continuation of the liberal arts tradition in twenty-first-century education.

Detweiler's study shows that an education in the liberal arts does not require students to forgo their aspirations for financial success. Educators need to subvert the false dichotomy between broad, formative learning and gainful employment. Moreover, we need to broach the topic of financial security just as we would other, less practical goods of the liberal arts to demonstrate that personal success is indeed a legitimate expectation students may have as they consider the kind of institution and program they want. Additionally, we need to recognize that professional training should and often does incorporate liberal arts principles; we can find ways to learn from these programs and collaborate with those who teach in and administer them. Detweiler pointedly argues that it is a "grave error" to abandon the liberal arts tradition and that doing so "destroy[s] higher education's long-term, constructive impact on graduates' lives and society." Given that personal success has proven to be one of the strongest motivators for students' pursuit of higher education, emphasizing the profitability of the liberal arts may be one of the most powerful ways to preserve and continue this tradition.

Why Liberal Arts Matter in Hiring

Don Eben

OVER THE YEARS, while working in positions ranging from manager to CEO, I have interviewed and hired many different people for various types and levels of positions. The common wisdom for hiring is to clarify the experience you are seeking, and then interview potential hires to see how closely their backgrounds match that experience. In other words, list the job requirements for the position, then ask questions in the interview process that allow the candidate to demonstrate those skills. This is not a bad process, but in my experience it misses key features that comprise a strong employee: a love for learning, an ability to solve problems, and effective communication skills.

Let me relay a specific example. At one company I was hired to take over two underperforming groups. We determined that we would have to replace many of the existing staff. We started the process of rehiring with the traditional method mentioned above. We listed the job requirements and sought applicants. We received a decent number of interested applicants for each position with résumés that seemed to fit the positions. In every case, however, the applicants ended up failing the interview process. They were only able to demonstrate the step-by-step application of their experience, and they failed to imagine how to apply their skills in other contexts. They could walk through *what* tasks they had accomplished very well but couldn't demonstrate a true understanding of *why* they had made certain choices or worked in that way. Their lack of discernment meant they couldn't answer any questions that moved beyond their previous experience.

The process ended in frustration, and we decided to change our approach. Instead of sending skill sets to the staffing companies, we requested three more intangible things. We asked for someone who wants to learn, someone who can solve problems, and someone who can effectively communicate when receiving or relaying information. We revamped our interview questions to be able to confirm these skills. We had fewer applications and several unconventional résumés. We interviewed several people from this pool and hired one. That hire quickly became a star in the group, despite having been part of the team for a short time. The choice worked so well that we continued with our less specific, more intangible list to fill all the remaining positions. Both teams went from underperforming to star teams. The morale rose significantly, and I still hear from people ten years later how much they remember that time and enjoyed being part of the team that this method produced.

There are a mass of articles on the value of hiring liberal arts majors in business: they have the soft skills needed; they can adapt to a changing workplace; they can think outside of the modus operandi of business training. Our unusual hiring process identified candidates with this formation, and the team's success proved that the skills promoted through a liberal arts education are indeed critical to a thriving business.

Students educated in the liberal arts are taught how to inquire and ask questions. They not only learn information but also the skill of learning. They are more likely to maintain a joy for learning throughout their years in the workforce. Their enjoyment of the learning process enables them to successfully navigate the changes that are unavoidable.

Finally, liberal arts students are taught how to communicate well. They learn how to receive, analyze, and understand information as well as how to create and present it. Effective communication is vital to how an individual and team perform overall. Since this time, I have made those three skills an important part of the interview and selection process regardless of the level of the position or what other skills are important. I have seen much more consistent success in the individuals selected for the positions.

Aren't the Liberal Arts a Luxury?

The liberal arts are great for well-off, healthy, happy people. I have money problems, family problems, health problems – it's all very exhausting. I don't have the time or energy to devote to this kind of formation right now, or maybe ever.

Remembering a Mentor

Margarita Mooney Clayton

TEARS ROLLED DOWN MY CHEEKS, and I put my hand on the hand of my dying friend, Albert Raboteau, the esteemed professor of African American religion at Princeton University. Covered in a quilt with "Grandpa" stitched on it, my mentor, collaborator, and fellow sojourner in faith struggled to keep his eyes open and listen to me.

After not having seen Al for nearly two years, I was here. His wife had called me in early September 2021 to tell me that his battle with Parkinson's and dementia was nearing the end.

My voice cracking, I promised Al I'd keep teaching his books *Slave Religion* and *American Prophets*. I thanked him for taking me to coffee so many mornings after Mass at St. Paul's Catholic Church in Princeton.

Then, I chanted in English all of Psalm 50.

"Thank you," Al said.

"How can I pray for you?" I asked him.

Struggling to speak, Al replied, "Pray for others. Pray for the suffering."

Slowly he lifted his hand and set it on mine. I leaned over and kissed his forehead. Then I said three Hail Marys and departed.

Al died a few days later.

His final words to me – to put others' needs before our own and to have empathy with the suffering – echoed the feedback he had given me on my own writing during one of our first coffee meetings in 2015. Al read some of my reports on my ethnographic work among Haitian immigrants and my in-depth interviews with people who have suffered sexual abuse, mental illness, and addiction. While addressing these multifaceted social issues, I asked Al's advice on how to also paint a picture of the spiritual struggles and lofty desires of the people I met. Rather than advising me to remain a neutral outside observer – the more common approach in sociology or history – Al encouraged me to engage people's stories empathetically and grant people their own voices.

His beautiful writing in *Slave Religion* analyzes the historical forces of oppression slaves experienced and presents their voices, including oftentimes their authentic deep faith in the Christian gospel.[1] In that book, Al employs first-person narratives of slaves and explores their faith and their moral judgments of their conditions of oppression. His book is thus not just an exemplary historical account of slavery but a model of history as an act of "recovery, a humanistic effort to increase knowledge." Recovering the slaves' voices through spirituals and slave memoirs furthers the universal search for truth and wisdom. Al describes how "people who had been through fire and refined like gold reveal the capability of the human spirit not only to endure bitter suffering but also to resist and even transcend the persistent attempt of evil to strike it down."

Although some would claim that slaves were forced to convert to Christianity, Al wrote about instances of genuine conversion among slaves, times when "professed doctrine becomes internally real." Slaves saw their own struggles reflected in the exodus stories of the Old Testament. At times, slaves were even invited to preach to masters' households. Slaves' conversion experiences truly injected a feeling of new life in them, and their religious worship expressed the movement from sorrow to joy, from damnation to salvation. Genuine conversion to Christianity helped slaves keep their identities as persons, even while enduring subhuman treatment. Religious worship became a space for "meaning, freedom, and transcendence."

Other accounts of slavery and religion look for ways that religious belief and worship either led to political resistance to slavery or encouraged slaves to passively accommodate to political injustice. But Al wrote that resistance and accommodation were not the only two options. The third option was redemptive suffering, the idea that unjust suffering can become a way in which the divine enters into human history.

For example, Al wrote that "the meaning [of the spirituals] was not so much an answer to the problem of suffering as the acceptance of the sorrow and the joy inherent in the human condition and an affirmation that life in itself was valuable." He insists that religious life itself was a form of "slave agency not entirely reducible to the political." In fact, "the moral authority of the slaves' faith was grounded in their suffering."

In his memoir *A Sorrowful Joy*, Al recounts his own repentance and experience of God's mercy. And he was willing to extend that mercy to others. In a 2015 talk he gave on forgiveness in the African American religious tradition, Al shared his own struggles to forgive the white man who had murdered his father.[2]

Right now, many people suffer unjustly. Some voices cry out that we should express our anger and do everything we can to change our circumstances. Al knew that suffering touches every human life. He believed that the cross was a central mystery of Christianity. From his historical study and from his own life and faith, Al knew the potentially redemptive power of unjust suffering. He had a light that shone from his inner self out to the horizon, a light that illuminated human experiences of suffering with hope.

Liberating the Least of These

Brad East

> the leisure of mind
> to lean on the fence and simply look, and not feel
> the need to press for a subtext, being so rare.
> —Denise Levertov, "A Little Visit to Doves and
> Chickens"

LONG AGO ARISTOTLE OBSERVED that leisure is necessary for the good life because leisure is necessary for contemplation, and the good life is a contemplative one.[3] Whether that last premise is one we share, it is hard to argue with his basic point: to develop the habit of stopping to smell the roses – using that expression to stand in for all nonutilitarian pleasures – one must be *able* to pause and do as one pleases. This ability is not universally shared, nor was it in ancient Greece. Some work and others play; some labor and toil, that is, while others enjoy the spoils: reading a novel, attending a play, performing a symphony, sketching a portrait, scribbling a poem. So if we are going to celebrate the goodness of the liberal arts, we have to be clear about whom we have in view. Everyone, or only some?

The first thing to note is the same point in reverse. If it is true that the liberal arts, broadly construed, are necessary for the good life, and if leisure is necessary to partake of the liberal arts, then it follows that leisure, in some measure and to some degree, should be available to all. Politics thus sneaks in through the back door the very moment we begin speaking of the liberal arts. They are liberal because they are for free women and men. But if women and men are not free, we do not jettison the arts. We jettison the chains that keep people unfree – in this case, unable to share in the higher goods that enrich and ennoble human life.[4]

The arts are capable of liberating us, then, because the deep, insatiable desire that draws us to these goods has the power, in turn, to eliminate obstacles to finding these goods, enjoying them, and using them to see the world and to bless our neighbors.

However, even if liberty were secured for everyone to partake in the arts, as individuals and as a community, no society is capable of ensuring that all have *equal* access to them, much less equal aptitude for their use or their enjoyment. Moreover, the circumstances of life intrude on even the most aesthetically attuned soul. To put it bluntly, then: Are the liberal arts for the wretched of the earth? For the damned and condemned and downtrodden? For the poor, the sick, the imprisoned? For the least of these? Or are they, like leisure for Athenian aristocrats, only for the well-off, the well-to-do, the able-bodied, the healthy, the happy, the emotionally and psychologically and relationally prosperous?

I see no reason to believe that our answer to this last question should be yes.

FIRST, CONSIDER THE POEM I quoted above. "A Little Visit to Doves and Chickens" describes that very thing: for twenty-four lines, it is nothing but a wryly admiring portrait of these birds, some above, some below, as though occupying "a two-storey house." And then the poet, Denise Levertov, comments:

> No, there's no moral nor irony
> lurking among these words, no message—
> unless the sense
>> that it's pleasant to visit a while
>> a modest, indeed a minute, poultry yard
>> where such content may be witnessed
>> and even a pair of guineafowl don't seem nervous
> is itself a message simply because
> it's wistful, the leisure of mind
> to lean on the fence and simply look, and not feel
> the need to press for a subtext, being so rare.[5]

Like every good poet, Levertov wants to have it both ways. And so she does. Her visit to the poultry yard is nothing but itself. It is not a text whose author has deposited esoteric meanings in between the lines. It is the unself-conscious life of creation, visited by a witness.

Yet the presence of the witness makes a difference. You and I were not there. Although she denies it, Levertov does draw a "moral" or "message" or "subtext" from the scene: namely, that the natural world is a reminder that sometimes presence is enough; no more is necessary. In a word, not every pastoral landscape is a poem. The moral is that, in order to be meaningful, you don't need a moral.

Except that Levertov finds a moral, making a text out of the yard-that-is-no-text, a poem from the just-a-landscape-not-a-poem. In doing so, she draws our attention to the myriad moments in our daily lives that are *not* rendered in masterly poetry, in which we nevertheless *ought* to be present, forsaking the quest for a lesson. By adorning her experience with words, she has created both a window and a mirror: a window – for us to look through, with her, at a certain time and place, seeing what she saw, hearing what she heard, mediated by her slanting lines; a mirror – for us to see our own world afresh, a world rarely if ever mediated by anything but our own senses, souls, minds, and paltry speech. In effect, she has consecrated our unpoetic lives by the art of her vision: a little visit to doves and chickens.

LEVERTOV'S WORK EMBODIES the rule that poetry, like all the arts, is not about some other life, in some other world; it's about us. It's subject matter is all-encompassing: humankind and all things in relation thereto. That's a bit like the definition of theology, which is the knowledge of God and all things in relation to God. Rightly, then, are the liberal arts also called the *humanistic* arts. The spirit that animates them is that of Terence: *Homo sum, humani nihil a me alienum puto.* Rendered loosely, the axiom says that if you are human, nothing human is finally alien to you.

In his book *Between the World and Me*, Ta-Nehisi Coates makes an important point along these lines: although the humanistic arts are by and for human beings, they are always located in particular cultures among particular peoples. This is a good thing, for human beings are not generic creatures; they are always concretely situated, clothed in cultural flesh and blood. The gift of Babel is a world of human difference. The curse of Babel appears when difference is perceived as threat, rather than gift.[6] Here we find artifacts of culture jealously hoarded and kept from others. We find, in Patrick Kavanagh's words, provincial rather than parochial culture.[7]

For example, Coates calls attention to the anecdote attributed to Saul Bellow: "Who is the Tolstoy of the Zulus?"[8] The quip is a taunt to anyone of African ancestry. *We* (Europeans? Russians? Judeo-Christians?) have an inheritance of incalculable value; what have *you*? Ralph Wiley's reply is the right one: "Tolstoy is the Tolstoy of the Zulus." "Unless," Coates wryly qualifies, "you find a profit in fencing off universal properties of mankind into exclusive tribal ownership." Wiley's riposte was a balm to Coates's insecurity in the face of Bellow's insult; it helped him realize that "Bellow was no closer to Tolstoy than I was to [seventeenth-century African queen] Nzinga. And if I were closer it would be because I chose to be, not because of destiny written in DNA."[9]

To be clear, the upshot is not that Tolstoy belongs to no one and thus to everyone. It is that Tolstoy – because his work, Russian and Christian and nineteenth-century to the marrow, has been received as a gift by times and places and peoples not his own – now belongs to others, indeed to any who take up his books and read them. For the gift of his work is neither regulated nor fungible. Once given, it cannot be ungiven; once received, it cannot be restricted, as if it were meant only for certain people and not others. Tolstoy is the Tolstoy of the Zulus.

Consider another example, one closer to (my) home. I live in west Texas. Every June for more than three decades, my university campus has hosted the Abilene Shakespeare Festival. Now ask yourself this question: What possible connection could the city and people of Abilene, Texas, have to the Globe Theatre in London, where the plays of the English playwright William Shakespeare were first performed more than four centuries ago?

Yes, we share a language. Yes, our nation has roots in England. Yes, the art of drama all over the world owes many debts to Shakespeare.

Such modest connections, though, are not sufficient to explain the annual Abilene Shakespeare Festival. The truth is that the festival exists because, believe it or not, in dry, dusty, scorching west Texas there are people who love Shakespeare as if he were their own. And he is. He is, for the simple reason that they love him and therefore keep his work alive. They love him enough to pour time, money, and talent into a yearly production that is free to the public, many of whom have never seen a performance of Shakespeare before they attend.

Who is the Shakespeare of the Texans? Shakespeare is the Shakespeare of the Texans.

EXAMPLES LIKE THESE could be multiplied. Dorothy L. Sayers's famous essay "Are Women Human?" comes to mind,[10] where she argues for the validity of women studying classics and philosophy. Granted, not all women (just like not all men) want to study Aristotle, but Sayers did; shouldn't she be able to? Aristotle is the Aristotle of women.

But the universality of the liberal arts is not the only question. Their reach is indeed universal, because they are human; and what is human belongs by definition to all human persons and peoples, provided they receive and enjoy any particular cultural gift as the gift that it is. The further question is whether such an exchange of gifts remains rarefied, fit primarily or exclusively for an upper class; if not a socioeconomic class, then at least a stratum of persons blessedly free, for a period of time or their whole lives, of the slings and arrows of illness, penury, pain, and loss. In other words, even if the liberal arts are for everyone in principle, can only a few receive them? Are they for every time and circumstance or just for everyone who has the time and whose circumstances are not dire?

I am a theologian, so theological examples come to mind. Consider two famous ones. The first is Boethius, an eminent thinker and writer who finds himself, in the early sixth century, arrested and imprisoned, awaiting death. To whom does he turn for consolation? None other than Lady Philosophy, who (he writes in *De consolatione philosophiae*) visits him in prison and provides the true medicine for his wounds. Here is a man, life and reputation destroyed, all earthly hopes lost, who has nothing to look forward to except his own impending execution – and he turns to what we would call "the classics." Not only does he find nourishment in them, he adds to their store. He writes his own dialogue for the sake of posterity. His consolation becomes a consolation to others yet unborn.[11]

About a century earlier, in North Africa, an aged bishop lies on his deathbed. Here is what his friend and fellow bishop writes of him:

> This is what he did in his own last illness: for he had ordered the four psalms of David that deal with penance to be copied out. From his sick-bed he could see these sheets of paper every day, hanging on his walls, and would read them, crying constantly and deeply. And, lest his attention be distracted from this in any way, almost ten days before his death, he asked us that none should come in to see him, except at those hours when the doctors would come to examine him or his meals were brought. This was duly observed: and so he had all that stretch of time to pray.[12]

The dying man is Saint Augustine. One might interpret his final days as a sort of expulsion or purging of all that has made him great, especially his vast learning: he is alone, like Boethius, away from his books, away from others' books, away from anything that might tempt him to pride, away from anyone but the Lord. In this way, perhaps, he seeks to enter the next life as a humble sinner rather than as a world-famous writer, teacher, and pastor. As Saint Thomas Aquinas would later comment about his own work: "It is only so much straw."[13]

Yet notice that Augustine is not in fact alone. Another sits by his bedside: not Lady Philosophy but King David.

The penitential psalms of David hang before his eyes, and he reads them over and over, as though he had not already memorized them decades before. The voice of the *Confessions*, after all, is as much David's as it is Augustine's. Augustine is not unaccompanied in his passing from this life to the next. David is there to shepherd him through.

It should not surprise us that Augustine chose psalms to keep him company in his final hours. In this he is, again, far from alone. How many times have psalms been read over a sick or dying soul? How many times at a funeral? Their spiritual power and aptness to the moment are much of the reason why. But Levertov would have us see the obvious: the psalms are poetry.[14] When the psalms of David are read in hospital rooms and at gravesides, at the outer limits of our suffering and grief, what we are hearing – and often, what we are pleading with – is poems. This is no accident.

Rowan Williams has observed that poetry, like theology, is language under pressure.[15] Poetry at its best, Williams writes, is "deployed as a means of exploration, invoking associations which may be random in one way, yet generate a steady level of unsettling alternative or supplementary meanings in the margin of the simple lexical sense."[16] Likewise theology, understood as any attempt to speak of God, is essentially exploratory, for it speaks of that which supersedes speech by definition. This doesn't mean we are thereby reduced to silence. But it does mean, oddly enough, that speech about God "is least off the mark when we are furthest from anything that looks like a fully coherent schema. Which is not an excuse for slackness, but an implicit plea for our words about God to be – as it were – carefully calculated shocks."[17] In the margins and indirections of poetry and theology alike, therefore, "we are not seeking a silence that will deliver us from the specificity of the world we inhabit but one that obliges an ever-deeper attention to it."[18] The mystery of the ineffable does not repulse us. It draws us in: further up and further in, as C. S. Lewis puts it.[19] For the journey deeper is without end.

Our original question should then be turned on its head. Given the fact that people yearn for poetry, as they yearn for God, in their times of greatest need or sorrow – since, put differently, we reach for *words* under pressure when our *lives* are under pressure – who would ever think the liberal arts are only for the good times? The consolations and catharsis of philosophy and poetry, psalms and prayers, drama and fiction, film and music speak to us most powerfully in the valley, not on the mountaintop. The shadow of death hangs over every one of our lives. The arts are a light. And, it would not be wrong to add, the darkness has not overcome it.

NOW, NO ONE WOULD CONTEST that ordinary people encounter the intellectual and fine arts in popular forms. People watch TV, listen to music, hang art on their walls. Rare is the person to whom this does not apply. All of us share in the arts in general. But do all of us find ways to participate in and benefit from art that is not superficial? The liberal arts have a vital, rather than a merely ornamental, role in our lives if and when they direct us to what transcends us, whereas art that is cheap, glib, ugly, or banal does not.[20]

Zena Hitz, in her book *Lost in Thought: The Hidden Pleasures of an Intellectual Life*, writes on this theme:

> When we act wholesomely we reach for something beyond, something more. We reach past the artificially induced tears of the theatrical production for wisdom about life, past sensual pleasure to intimacy with another human being, past grief over a loss to gratitude and renewal of purpose. That is how human beings are meant to function, how things work when all is going well. Unless we treasure something beyond our own bare experience, we cannot distinguish gazing at a mighty river from gazing at the TV channels changing one to the other, over and over again.[21]

It is important to see that the object of Hitz's critique is not the simple pleasures of popular art forms. Instead, it is the temptation to remain at the surface of things. But there is art that induces such a tendency within us. Call it art of the spectacle, which forms our hearts and minds *not* to expect anything more than "bare experience."

By contrast, there is art that points us to "something beyond," though just how to represent that relationship is a perennial question facing any artist. This is why Josef Pieper connects work to leisure, leisure to culture, culture to worship, and the seamless whole – leisure/culture/ worship – to ecstasy. Together they set us outside ourselves. Precisely in attending to what is altogether human, the arts signify what is more than human. As Pieper writes:

Leisure is a form of silence, of that silence which is the prerequisite of the apprehension of reality: only the silent hear and those who do not remain silent do not hear. Silence, as it is used in this context, does not mean "dumbness" or "noiselessness"; it means more nearly that the soul's power to "answer" to the reality of the world is left undisturbed. For leisure is a receptive attitude of mind, a contemplative attitude, and it is not only the occasion but also the capacity for steeping oneself in the whole of creation.[22]

We have come full circle, to the "leisure of mind" a society must, in justice, provide to all, and to the silence that empowers vision: namely, to see doves and chickens for what they are, and not only what they might be for me.

I'll close with an example of this sort of vision, one that sees beyond by quite literally seeing through. On September 15, 1963, a bomb was detonated inside the Sixteenth Street Baptist Church in Birmingham, Alabama. The bomb was planted there by a splinter group of the KKK, who set it to go off during services that Sunday morning. Four Black schoolgirls died. Across the Atlantic Ocean, a Welsh artist named John Petts heard the news and wanted to respond. He started a campaign to raise funds across Wales, stipulating that only small donations would be accepted, to ensure the funds would come from common people and not merely a few wealthy patrons. In less than two years, a new stained-glass window was installed in the Birmingham church, and it remains there to this day.[23]

The window portrays Christ, depicted as a Black man, arms outstretched simultaneously in the traditional *orans* prayer position and in a cruciform shape. His halo is a rippling multicolored rainbow. He is not dead; he is not yet beyond pain. It is as though he is being assailed or accosted, but standing firm. His head is bowed, but he will not be moved.

At the bottom of the window a text reads, YOU DO IT TO ME, echoing the words of Jesus in the twenty-fifth chapter of Matthew's Gospel. The window is a gift, from one people to another. It is a work of insight, one people – unknown to the other – seeing in them what even next-door neighbors, blinded by race, could not see. What they saw was human beings, suffering unjustly; accordingly, they saw Christ. The artwork produced as a result enacts and encourages this double vision: to see more than can be seen by the senses, to spy in the margins something overlooked, to administer a carefully calculated shock.

Liberation from Lonely Suffering and Death

Lydia S. Dugdale

THE ACUTE AWARENESS of human finitude that comes when one knows one is dying usually prompts a host of actions: reconciliation with God or fellow mortals, review of last will and testament, distribution of keepsakes. For some the turn is more poetic. Boethius penned dialogues as he awaited his execution. Augustine meditated on the Psalms. None of this should surprise us. As Brad East puts it, "The consolations and catharsis of philosophy and poetry, psalms and prayers, drama and fiction, film and music speak to us most powerfully in the valley, not on the mountaintop." The liberal arts liberate our souls amidst tragedy, sickness, and despair. The arts gift us the possibility of transformation.

This might seem a foregone conclusion for anyone reading this page. But what of those who cannot read, for want of vigor or vitality? What of those who can't partake of the liberal arts? What about patients dying in the intensive care unit, unable to speak because they're unable to breathe without the miracle of modern mechanical ventilation? What about those whose cognition has long since taken leave, whose worlds have contracted to include the few nameless but hopefully pleasant-enough caregivers who feed, bathe, and clothe them? What do the liberal arts do for them?

The answer, perhaps plainly enough, is that the liberal arts were never meant to be contemplated, enjoyed, or experienced in total isolation. The people of Abilene, Texas, host a Shakespeare festival because it is the *collective* that is meant to share Shakespeare. Similarly, symphonies sound, painters paint, and poets compose for audiences. The production, reception, and digestion of the humanities is meant to take place in the community. What good is Julius Caesar's pronouncement, "Seeing that death, a necessary end / Will come, when it will come," if Caesar is the last person standing?[24] Even though Shakespeare's Caesar is speaking to his wife Calpurnia, his speech is intended also for the audience. If the arts prompt us to reflect on what it means to be mortal, and if to be human is to be in relationship, then the arts are for humanity.

But that still doesn't answer the question of the unconscious ventilated patient or the forgotten silent elderly. What do the liberal arts do for those who cannot actively participate? Here, the *ars moriendi* tradition offers one response.

During the aftermath of the devastating mid-1300s bubonic plague outbreak in western Europe, priests were at an all-time low, and the laity expressed misgivings about their own ability to prepare well for death. Such tasks, after all, belonged to the learned and the clergy. What was the common person to do should plague recur, war break out, or famine descend?

In response, social authorities, likely affiliated with the Council of Constance, circulated a handbook on preparation for death called the *Tractatus artis bene moriendi*, or "Treatise on the Art of Dying Well." This small book not only provided the laity with the tools they needed to anticipate their mortality and prepare, it also equipped them to intercede on behalf of the dying who were no longer able to do the work themselves.

What might this look like? For starters, the handbook provided instruction on encouragement of the dying and a catechism that community members could use to ask questions to confirm the faith of the dying person. But for those unable even to speak, the *ars moriendi* provided prayers that the healthy could utter on behalf of the dying. The art of dying thus proposed a collective solution to the problem of isolated inability to participate. The need to prepare for death is universal, and this first handbook eventually spawned a genre of such books that circulated widely for more than five centuries.

Physicians and scientists are only just beginning to understand the extent to which seemingly unconscious patients can process conversation directed toward them.[25] In what is now termed "disorders of consciousness," some nonresponsive patients demonstrate appropriate responses on brain imaging or electroencephalogram (EEG), even if their bodies physically show no response. Patients with so-called "covert awareness" are more likely to recover than those without. Why does this matter to those who are reading a book on the liberal arts? Because it suggests that those in our midst who seem unaware of their living or dying may be more engaged than we are inclined to believe.

It is common that as dementia advances, individuals so affected stop speaking or eating. This is a natural course for the cognitive disease. In my book *The Lost Art of Dying*, I write about an occasion when I was able to witness a music therapist visiting one such patient:

> She could not get out of bed, rarely opened her eyes, and had to be spoon-fed. She never, ever spoke. Family members told the therapist, a violinist, that "Amazing Grace" had been one of the woman's favorite songs. As the violin released the notes of that quiet, hopeful melody, the old woman opened her mouth and began to sing, her voice cracking yet steady, mostly on pitch. She could no longer talk. But she could sing.[26]

When shared, the liberal arts have the power to liberate us from our isolating frailty and draw us back into the embrace of community.

Despite more than six million deaths globally from Covid-19 and a devastating war in Ukraine, among other threats to human existence, those living in the affluent West remain particularly uneasy about reckoning with their own finitude or the deaths of loved ones. But we doubtless would be less prone to fear the valley of the shadow of death were we to exchange our daily meditations of newsfeeds and social media for the "consolations and catharsis" of the liberal arts of dying.

Aren't the Liberal Arts Just for Smart People?

A liberal arts education sounds great for exceptionally smart people. I am just a normal person; I don't think I'm eligible. Anyway, those who work with their hands or stay home to raise children don't really need the liberal arts.

Lyceums: Places to Think with Neighbors

Nathan Beacom

IN 1826, IN CONNECTICUT, a farmer named Josiah Holbrook started a school for "the general diffusion of knowledge and . . . raising the moral and intellectual taste" of Americans.[1] In those days, the opportunities for higher education were limited to those venerable old universities that had long served the upper crust. Holbrook's vision was to make learning – practical, liberal, and humane – available to working people of all kinds. He named his school the Lyceum, after the garden where Aristotle once taught his students philosophy.

The idea spread like wildfire. Within a few decades, there were thousands of Lyceums across the country, representing a thriving intellectual life in large cities and small country towns. Abraham Lincoln gave his first public speech at a Lyceum in Springfield, Illinois. Frederick Douglass, Mark Twain, Susan B. Anthony, and all the great thinkers of the day toured the Lyceum circuit, putting their ideas in dialogue with ordinary Americans. Everything Henry David Thoreau wrote was for his local Lyceum in Concord. When Alexander Graham Bell debuted the telephone, it was at a Lyceum. In Jefferson, Iowa, or Brookline, Massachusetts, you could find working folks listening to lectures on anthropology, philosophy, politics, and more. And then the Lyceum disappeared. Communities broke apart in the Gilded Age as families moved and shifted toward big cities. Individualism replaced the communal learning of the past and social Darwinism became the new philosophy du jour. In reaction to growing individualism and weakening community life, grassroots organizations were formed to knit communities back together, like the Rotary Club, Kiwanis Club, Lions, and others. Protestant Americans emphasized the "social gospel," and Catholics introduced the language of "social justice." Lyceums, too, saw a revival in the form of the Public Forum Movement. These and other factors contributed to historically high levels of social trust and civic participation in the middle of the twentieth century.

But, as social scientist Robert Putnam has famously documented, social cohesion, community engagement, and community trust have plummeted across a wide array of measures since that time, and these things have taken a nosedive from the 1990s to now.[2] People report fewer conversations with neighbors, fewer friendships, less engagement in community organizations and civic life, and a growing distrust of their fellow Americans. Coincident with all this, our engagement with ideas has moved away from a public forum with neighbors and toward TV and social media, where the humanizing element of physical proximity is lost. No longer are we in the scrum of intellectual engagement with those with whom we live; instead, we are locked in our own angry echo chambers online, growing ever more extreme and unable to sympathize with those unlike us.

In this environment, the Lyceum Movement has launched an effort to bring back this forum for conversation and learning. In its time, the Lyceum was a way for neighbors to form relationships around a common pursuit of learning. This is eminently good for a community. In the process of shared learning and intellectual exploration, trust and shared understanding grow, and a habit of cooperation in search of a shared good, the good of knowledge, is formed.

In the midst of a confusing turmoil of online noise, the Lyceum offers a place to think about first principles and about the stories we share. We hold lectures, panels, classes, and community conversation in a relaxed social atmosphere. Human beings have always needed this, whether in the Greek agora or a Boston tavern; we need a place to pursue the fundamental human desire *to know* with our neighbors.

Since its beginning in 2021, the new Lyceum Movement has grown to a presence in four states and six cities, and it has generated a remarkable amount of positive energy in communities large and small. People are hungry for an alternative to the alienating experience of life online; they're hungry for a substantive conversation with a neighbor.

We take the subjects of the liberal arts and put them in local contexts. In Des Moines, Iowa, we've spoken about virtue ethics by way of a discussion between commodity farmers and farmers focused on sustainability. We've explored questions of human solidarity through dialogue between philosophers and refugees. We've explored local history in places like Duluth, Minnesota, and Saint Louis, Missouri. These are subjects many people think about in the quiet moments of their working lives, and they are hungry for an opportunity to develop those thoughts with the help of a scholar or expert and in conversation with their neighbors. This is often true of those who don't suspect that this kind of intellectual talk is for them. Not everyone is an academic, nor should they be, and our events have been places where a farmer, a construction worker, a lawyer, and a schoolteacher can think deeply together.

A healthy common life requires a shared frame of reference, a shared language, and a shared sense of purpose. If we only talk as a community at times of political conflict, we are bound to talk past each other. We won't have a shared understanding of the very words we are using, we won't have shared stories to point to, and we won't have relationships of trust to ground us. The liberal arts can offer something here. Studying philosophy, literature, and history in community can at least give us a common set of terms, a better understanding of our neighbor's point of view, and a shared frame of reference so that we can fruitfully disagree.

We need to go deeper than the superficial fights that characterize our public life. We need to return to first principles and meet each other there as human beings. The Lyceum is working to provide a space to do this, with the goal of bringing back the Lyceum Halls that once served as the center of community learning and thinking for so many cities. Learning in community is not a panacea for our complex problems, but it can help cultivate the soil from which productive work for the common good may grow.

Liberal Learning for All

Jessica Hooten Wilson

"**A**LL HUMANS BY NATURE desire to know." So begins Aristotle's *Metaphysics*.[3] Knowing is not an activity for the few but a desire shared by all. It's where we get the definition of human beings as *homo sapiens*; we are knowing creatures, preferably wise ones. The lie that convinces people that certain knowledge is reserved for only a handful threatens to rob humans of their birthright. Dystopian novels show us what happens when the great majority of people rescind their invitation to knowledge in exchange for entertainment and economic security. When liberal arts are relegated from universal and freeing ways of knowing to the purview of eggheads, everyone else loses out.

In the nineteenth century, Anna Julia Cooper was born a slave in America but rose up through liberal arts education to be the fourth African American woman to receive a PhD, from the Sorbonne, no less. When she taught school and served as a principal, managing the curriculum of an all-Black high school, she rejected the idea that liberal arts were merely for the elite. Cooper responded to the sneer of those who asked what good this education would do Black people by answering, "The aim for education for the human soul is to train aright, to give power and right direction to the intellect, the sensibilities and the will." [4] These were not mere hands she was responsible for schooling; her students had heads and hearts to be cultivated. A century later, however, the attitude that Cooper rejected has become more prevalent. Now people ask, "What good is this education for a future nurse? An engineer? A businessman? A woman who plans to stay home as a mother?" Cooper was adamant that the liberal arts were building "not chemists or farmers or cooks, or soldiers, but [people] ready to serve the body politic in whatever avocation their talent is needed." [5] In order to do so well, educators must see past the false assumption that a liberal arts education is a nice luxury for the privileged few rather than a set of essential capacities for everyone.

For Cooper, education was not merely the training of the hands – what we might erroneously call vocational training – but should include "head, hand, and heart." She believed education was for the "mind, body, and spirit": "We must, whatever else we do, insist on those studies, which by the consensus of educators are calculated to train our people to think, which will give them the power of appreciation and make them righteous." [6] Cooper does not explicitly write truth, beauty, and goodness, but those are the three ends implied by the verbs thinking, appreciating, and being righteous. In a liberal education of the sort that Cooper describes, the person seeks knowledge not for power, economic success, or egoistic self-improvement but for the love of higher ends. Understood this way, liberal arts become the training for a rightly ordered and embodied soul, what we might call a "well-rounded person." (I personally disdain that idiom, which always makes me imagine Violet Beauregarde blowing up like a blueberry in Roald Dahl's *Charlie and the Chocolate Factory*!)

The Liberal Arts Are *Arts*

We misunderstand the role of liberal arts when we consider them in terms of their useful skills and content rather than as ways of knowing. To circle back to Aristotle (he was really smart, so even if it seems clichéd to cite him, we shouldn't ignore him), he identifies three ways of knowing: *praxis* (doing), *poiesis* (making), and *theoria* (contemplating). Where would the average person assume the liberal arts fit? Many people assume liberal arts are ethereal, so they might categorize them as *theoria*. However, the trivium (grammar, logic, rhetoric) and quadrivium (arithmetic, geometry, music, astronomy) are *arts*, meaning *poiesis*. We *make* in the liberal arts: we are culture makers. Without liberal arts education, we make poor culture.

J. Scott Lee writes of the necessity of returning *art* to our understanding of liberal arts, drawing from Aristotle's definition. In *Invention: The Art of Liberal Arts*, Lee writes, "For Aristotle, art is a cause of things coming into being in this world that, otherwise, would not exist without active human agency. It touches our deepest natures and desires, and it exercises our minds and passions to a degree of inventiveness that our imaginations struggle to keep up with, incorporates almost anything that the universe has to offer, and results in a changed world that, without art, would be barren."[7] Several notable authors have written about human beings as culture makers (Makoto Fujimura, Andy Crouch, Dorothy L. Sayers).[8] To be one who makes is not an exceptional calling but a universal vocation rooted in our nature as humans made in the image of God. We make gardens, books, inventions, food, communities – and finally a life. The liberal arts teach us how to make what is worth making, in part by drawing from our past and speaking to our future.

These Arts Are Liberating

If the meaning of liberal arts as *arts* been misconstrued, the meaning of "liberal" is also lost on most people. We hear the word, and we think of politics or morals. We conflate "liberal" with "libertarian" or "progressive." However, the word means *free*, from the Latin *liberalis*. The liberal arts are those that free a person to make, without the constraints of coercion, consumerism, or ideology. While human societies usually suffer from various systems of oppression or economic disparities, liberal arts free human persons to pursue more generative modes of making. Persons so formed are freed as much *from* societal ills as *for* the good life.

When a group of liberal arts professors gathered together virtually at the start of the 2020 pandemic, we discussed what to call our motley crew. We settled on "The Liberating Arts" as a way of emphasizing the definition of "liberal" found in "liberal arts." While the adjective had lost its edge in contemporary discourse, we hoped revising it to "liberating" would revitalize the phrase, showing the power the liberal arts make available to those who practice them. This word also signifies how freedom becomes compelling: the free person desires to liberate others, including future generations. An exemplar in this endeavor is the young man who once believed that the shadows in Plato's cave composed all of reality; once he was freed from the cave to see real things, he returned to call others out from their imprisonment in shadowland.

The free soul is not an autonomous individual indulging in licentious hedonism; rather, the free soul is an interdependent person among persons, controlling his or her appetites for the good of other people and for the good of the land and its other inhabitants. Using this freedom well, this person will form friendships rather than networks, investigate the truth without fear, love the beautiful, and find happiness in goodness.

Liberal Education versus Liberal Arts Schooling

To categorize the liberal arts as a luxury for the rich and nerdy is to miss out on the education that so many have fought for, particularly women and African Americans. What was once held out of reach is now widely available, yet despite being accessible, it's not sufficiently desired and pursued. In 1971 the public intellectual Ivan Illich warned the world that the mass schooling system – public education – would confuse "teaching with learning, grade advancement with education, a diploma with competence, and fluency with the ability to say something new."[9] His caution proved prophetic. We now think of education as getting a diploma, hence the more popular term "graduation" instead of "commencement." No longer does education provide the beginning of a path; now we settle for the conferring of a degree. We focus on grades, résumés, certificates, micro and macro credentialing. Learning the art of being free human beings does not fit within this narrative.

Illich foresaw how the institutionalization of school would lead to the degradation of education, that job training would replace culture making. In *Deschooling Society* (1971), after forecasting this grim future, he briefly offers an alternative: "What kinds of things and people might learners want to be in contact with in order to learn?"[10] He proposes four resources: the things themselves (nature, books, art), models (from whom we might learn), peers (with whom we dialogue), and elders (those who see the historical context and have the experiential wisdom to lead us). Liberal arts education does not require a classroom; rather, it prioritizes those four resources. Draw a model into conversation with peers and elders to discuss a thing, and you have liberal arts education. No institution is required.

Institutions began as a way of opening the door more broadly, to encourage those without the same resources or background as the upper middle class to access liberal arts education. Many of the universities that the contributors to this book have worked for began as missionary enterprises. Even now, if colleges and universities were to reinvest in the liberal arts as necessary to their mission, they could be fruitful places. Within their walls, eager students would easily find mentors; the structure of a program unburdens the student from planning a course of study; and the institution could be a beacon for the potential of liberal arts formation. However, with or without institutions, liberal arts education is fundamental for forming civil amateurs – or lovers – of truth, goodness, and beauty.

Against Specialization

Those who assume that only a few should cultivate the liberal arts are thinking within a paradigm of specialization: let the English majors take the writing classes and the music majors enjoy their Bach. Despite the trends in education that push specialization, the data suggest that more time in general liberal arts education provides higher vocational success and longer staying power within a chosen field.[11] Liberal arts training affects people's ability to reason, persevere, love, and enjoy. None of these requires specialization or is the purview of only a few. When you study biology in college as a business major, you are not aiming to specialize. You have no idea how the training will assist you in your life. Liberal arts education forms you beyond the parameters of your work.

In his 2019 book *Range: Why Generalists Triumph in a Specialized World*, David Epstein builds a case for liberal arts education, emphasizing the benefits of generalized education – why it's good for future scientists to study poetry and doctors to learn history. In one chapter, "Thinking outside Experience," he shows how Johannes Kepler relied on his knowledge of analogies to conceive of the right model for space. Through its very form, poetry increases such analogical thinking. Elsewhere in the book Epstein relates a 1930s thought experiment by Karl Duncker, in which doctors face a patient whose tumor seems inoperable. By recalling a historical anecdote of a general moving his troops to attack a fortress, the doctors could see outside the limits of their expertise to find a solution to treating the tumor. The book is overflowing with such examples of the ways in which we cannot quantify liberal arts learning even as we experience its benefits in how we live and work.[12]

Ending with Aristotle

We began with Aristotle, so let's end with his wisdom. His view of education centralized the master-disciple relationship that he had experienced with Plato and that Plato formed with Socrates. We might also think of the disciples and Jesus. Or the monks around Hugh of Saint-Victor. And so on. Illich quotes Aristotle to explain this view of education: "it makes a gift, or does whatever it does, as to a friend." This idea of education shows friends enjoying leisure (the Greek word is *schole*, from which we derive "school") to pursue ultimate human goods. Should not this be the picture of a good life – friends, in freedom, making culture? The liberal arts were never meant to be kept on a top shelf away from the majority. Rather, the liberal arts are liberating. Through mathematics, music, general sciences, and the humanities, we are formed more fully into the culture makers we desire to be. By their practice and content, the liberal arts teach us to love what is worth loving and to pass on that love to others in joy and friendship.

Small Magazines as Educational Communities

Peter Mommsen

"STUPIDITY IS THE GREATEST SIN" was a favorite saying of Eberhard Arnold, the German theologian and educator who, a century ago, founded the magazine I now edit. On its face, the statement sounds insufferable – how can someone's lack of intellectual gifts be cast as a moral failure? Interpreted this way, Arnold's one-liner comes across as a cruel dunk on the unlettered, the underprivileged, and the mentally slow.

But Arnold means something close to the opposite. Far from a slur denigrating those who lack a college degree or who score low on Raven's matrices, *stupidity* in his sense is a vice of complacency that particularly afflicts the educated bourgeoisie – the very people who make up the bulk of the readership of any small magazine.

What Arnold means by stupidity becomes clear from reviewing a sampling of the places he detected it. He saw stupidity, for instance, among many of his fellow intellectuals, "know-it-alls who can talk about everything but don't know how to do much of anything" and who acted superciliously toward the working class who did. He saw it among many of his fellow Christians, whose "self-centeredness and self-contemplation make the spirit stupid and dull." And he saw it in the National Socialist regime that hounded him during the two years before his early death in 1935:

> Modern fascism is such that one could weep about it day and night. Freedom of thought is forbidden. Objective justice is abolished. Goebbels says, "If we are right, it follows that no one else is right. For us there is no other justice than that which serves our interests." Stupidity reigns.[13]

Whatever its manifestation, stupidity in Arnold's view stems from a choice: a refusal to take up the task that comes with being human, beginning with the refusal to know the truth about oneself. His maxim reflects a well-known aphorism coined by Nietzsche: "To forget one's purpose is the commonest form of stupidity."[14] The result is apathy – an insensitivity toward the true, the beautiful, and the good as they appear in the various spheres of life, from religion to politics to nature to the arts.

Accordingly, Arnold's mission as a writer and publisher amounted to an ardent campaign against stupidity. The magazine's task, he believed, was to stir people out of their self-satisfaction with a "summons" to "living renewal," as he put it in a 1920 editorial that still serves as the magazine's mission statement. This means inviting everyone, whether academically trained or not, into a life of continual learning within an "educational community," in which ancient wisdom is brought to bear on modern dilemmas: "We must get down to the deepest roots of Christianity and demonstrate that they are crucial to solving the urgent problems in contemporary culture. With breadth of vision and energetic daring, our publishing house must steer its course right into the torrent of contemporary thought."

This is a mission that remains as challenging today as ever, and just as crucial. The current incarnation of the publication Arnold founded is *Plough*. (Plough Publishing House also publishes a line of books, including the one you're holding in your hands.) Each issue is themed around a topic that its editors believe has pressing significance, such as capitalism, medicine, vocation, or faith and politics. The means are various: big essays, on-the-ground reporting, readings from classical and medieval authors, personal narratives, comics, poetry, and art and photography. The aim of small magazines like *Plough* is not simply to inform or entertain but to offer fresh perspectives that help readers think differently and equip them to live their lives more intentionally. Nor is that a one-way street: from readers who offer contrasting views, argue, critique, and sometimes unsubscribe, editors and writers can learn to see the world from perspectives they otherwise would have missed.

It's exhilarating to see the power of small magazines to draw together an unlikely assortment of thinkers, readers, and doers into the kind of educational communities that Arnold envisioned. A few publications that have been doing this well are *The Baffler, Comment, Commonweal, First Things, The Hedgehog Review, Jacobin, The Lamp, Local Culture, Mere Orthodoxy, Mockingbird, The New Atlantis,* and *The Point*. Increasingly, small magazines like these are facilitating local gatherings of their readers in various towns and cities, to build community though face-to-face conversation.

A common pitfall of the present moment is that any publication risks becoming predictably partisan and then being pigeonholed and dismissed as either right-wing or left-wing. It can be tough to resist the currents tugging a writer or an editor into an attitude that assumes an "us" while excluding a "them," or that simply serves up regular helpings of whatever kinds of hot take will reliably fire up one's base. I've found that a strong antidote is a rigorous commitment to seeking truth together with people with whom I disagree and an openness to discovering common ground in surprising places.

It's essential that this truth-seeking be rooted in a way of life – that we find ways to put the insights we gain into practice. Ultimately, it's within real, not virtual, communities that the lifelong learning of Arnold's "educational communities" can best be sustained. The small magazines I've just mentioned are each, in different ways, focal points for networks of people who want to not just think well, but do well. (Of course, they vary widely in their sense of what this actually looks like.)

To take *Plough* as the example I know best, this is a network of readers, writers, and practitioners drawn to the magazine for any number of reasons. From surveys, we know they span the political spectrum and hold a wide range of philosophical and religious beliefs. Yet they share a common conviction summed up by the magazine's motto: "Another life is possible."

Although today the word "community" carries a suspicious odor thanks to its abuse by corporate marketing departments, for the readership of a small magazine it's an accurate term. In the case of *Plough*'s staff, this is true even more literally: the same year that Arnold founded *Plough*, he also founded the Bruderhof, the Christian intentional community that publishes the magazine and of which many (but not all) of the editors are members. The flesh-and-blood communal life behind the magazine is proof that the collective task of discovering and remembering our purpose as human beings is not just an idealistic project but also an eminently practical one.

As it happens, this somewhat unusual case study provides substantiation, too, for the liberating arts' broader claim that the search for truth is not something reserved to the academically educated. To speak from my own experience, on the Bruderhof where I grew up, in New York's Hudson Valley, I got to know older members who were the evidence of this. There was the tool-and-die maker who loved Dostoyevsky, the sheep farmer who sang Schubert's *Lieder*, and the former factory worker who kept a copy of Kierkegaard on his coffee table. This was just what Arnold, who himself regularly spent time turning the communal farm's manure pile before heading to his study to write and edit, had in mind. From a 1920 essay:

> We should be ready to spend several hours each day (provided we are in good health) doing physical work. Intellectuals, in particular, would discover the wholesome effect this has. Daily practical work allows each person's special light, his or her particular gift, to be kindled. This spark in each one, though maybe hidden, gives a glimpse of various gifts – possibly in scholarship, music, the use of words, creative art in woodwork, sculpture, or painting. Or simplest

and best of all, a nature-loving person may have a particular gift for farm or garden work. . . . Idleness and tedium are symptoms of death. Where there is life, people have alert, creative minds and are ready to serve and help one another. This is not mere fantasy about an unattainable future; it is a present reality in a growing community.[15]

Such lifelong educational community, whatever the varying forms it may take, is the goal of the liberating arts. It's the way that we can remember our purpose as human beings possessing bodies, minds, and souls. And it's an effective answer to the stupidity that continues to afflict our world.

Contributors

Emily Auerbach is the executive director and co-founder of the Odyssey Project and a professor of English at the University of Wisconsin–Madison. She co-hosts Wisconsin Public Radio's *University of the Air.*

Nathan Beacom, a writer from Des Moines, Iowa, is the founder and executive director of the Lyceum Movement. His writing on agriculture, the environment, and other subjects has appeared in *Civil Eats, America Magazine, Front Porch Republic,* and *Plough.*

Jeffrey Bilbro is an associate professor of English at Grove City College and an editor at *Front Porch Republic.* He is the author of several books, most recently *Reading the Times: A Literary and Theological Inquiry into the News.*

Joseph Clair is an associate professor of ethics and the executive dean of the Cultural Enterprise at George Fox University. He is the author of several books including most recently, *Reading Augustine: On Education, Formation, Citizenship and the Lost Purpose of Learning.*

Margarita Mooney Clayton is an associate professor of practical theology at Princeton Theological Seminary, and the founder and director of the Scala Foundation. She is author of several books including *The Love of Learning: Seven Dialogues on the Liberal Arts* and *The Wounds of Beauty: Seven Dialogues on Art and Education.*

Lydia S. Dugdale is a physician and ethicist at Columbia University Vagelos College of Physicians and Surgeons, where she directs the Center for Clinical Medical Ethics. She is the author, most recently, of *The Lost Art of Dying: Reviving Forgotten Wisdom.*

Brad East is an associate professor of theology at Abilene Christian University. His writing has appeared in *Los Angeles Review of Books, Christian Century, Christianity Today, Comment, Commonweal, First Things, The Hedgehog Review, The New Atlantis, Plough,* and *The Point.*

Don Eben is the owner and CEO of Core Network Strategies, a telecommunications contracting corporation. An avid supporter of classical education, he serves on the board of Sager Classical Academy in Arkansas.

Becky L. Eggimann is Dean of Natural Sciences and an associate professor of biochemistry at Wheaton College.

Rachel B. Griffis is an associate professor of English at Spring Arbor University. She has written about American literature and Christian education in *Christianity and Literature, Christian Scholar's Review, The Cormac McCarthy Journal, Literature and Theology, Studies in American Indian Literatures,* and elsewhere.

David Henreckson is an assistant professor and Director of the Weyerhaeuser Center for Christian Faith and Learning at Whitworth University. He is author of *The Immortal Commonwealth,* a recipient of the Manfred Lautenschlaeger Award.

Zena Hitz is a tutor at St. John's College in Annapolis, as well as founder and president of the Catherine Project. She is the author of *Lost In Thought: The Hidden Pleasures of an Intellectual Life* and *A Philosopher Looks at the Religious Life.*

David Hsu is an associate professor and engineering program director at Wheaton College. He has worked in biomedical and telecom research and is now a mechanical engineering design consultant and researcher in the area of computational materials science.

L. Gregory Jones is currently the president of Belmont University. He was previously executive vice president and provost of Baylor University and dean of Duke Divinity School. He is the author of many books including *Navigating the Future: Traditioned Innovation for Wilder Seas.*

Brandon McCoy is a student at Harvard Law School. He has written several education policy issue briefs and opinion editorials on classical education, school choice, and civics.

Peter Mommsen is editor-in-chief of *Plough Quarterly* magazine and the author of *Homage to a Broken Man: The Life of J. Heinrich Arnold.*

Angel Adams Parham is the executive director of Nyansa Classical Community. She is an associate professor of sociology and a senior fellow at the Institute for Advanced Studies in Culture at the University of Virginia. Her books include *The Black Intellectual Tradition: Reading Freedom in Classical Literature.*

Steve A. Prince is a mixed media artist, master printmaker, lecturer, educator, and art evangelist. He is currently Director of Engagement and Distinguished Artist in Residence at the Muscarelle Museum at William and Mary University.

John Mark Reynolds is the president of the Saint Constantine School, a kindergarten-through-college program. Previously he was provost at Houston Baptist University and the founder of the Torrey Honors Institute at Biola University. His books include *When Athens Met Jerusalem: An Introduction to Classical and Christian Thought.*

Erin Shaw is a Chickasaw-Choctaw artist. She studied fine arts at Baylor University and the University of Oklahoma, and is now an assistant professor of visual arts at John Brown University.

Anne Snyder is the editor-in-chief of *Comment* and the founder of *Breaking Ground*, a collaboration of institutions with a Christian humanist approach. She hosts *The Whole Person Revolution* podcast and is the author of *The Fabric of Character: A Wise Giver's Guide to Renewing our Social and Moral Landscape*.

Sean Sword is a student majoring in criminology at Calvin University. A juvenile offender, he served twenty-seven years in prison and began his college studies at the Richard A. Handlon Correctional Facility in Ionia, Michigan, through the Calvin Prison Initiative.

Noah Toly is Provost at Calvin University. He is the author or editor of several books, most recently *The Gardeners' Dirty Hands: Environmental Politics and Christian Ethics*, which received the Aldersgate Prize.

Jonathan Tran is an associate professor of theology at Baylor University and an associate dean in its Honors College. He is the author of *Asian Americans and the Spirit of Racial Capitalism* and coeditor of the Oxford University Press book series Reflection and Theory in the Study of Religion.

Jessica Hooten Wilson is the inaugural Seaver College Scholar of Liberal Arts at Pepperdine University and a senior fellow at Trinity Forum. She is the author of several books, most recently *The Scandal of Holiness: Renewing Your Imagination in the Company of Literary Saints*.

Notes

1. What Are the Liberating Arts?

1 See Jeffrey Bilbro, "Going Dark," *Breaking Ground*, September 29, 2020.

2 Abraham Joshua Heschel, *The Sabbath* (New York: Farrar, Straus and Giroux, 2005 [1951]), 17–18.

3 Clare Coffey, Rob Sentz, and Yustina Saleh, "Degrees at Work: Examining the Serendipitous Outcomes of Diverse Degrees," EMSI Profile Analytics, August 2019.

4 Mark Schwehn, *Exiles from Eden: Religion and the Academic Vocation in America* (Oxford: Oxford University Press, 1993), 61.

2. Aren't the Liberating Arts a Waste of Time?

1 Augustine, *Confessions*, trans. Henry Chadwick (Oxford: Oxford University Press, 2009), 104 (6.11.18).

2 Augustine, *Confessions*, 92–3 (6.3.3).

3 Ambrose, *Concerning Virginity*, trans. H. de Romestin, E. de Romestin and H.T.F. Duckworth, in *Nicene and Post-Nicene Fathers, Second Series*, Vol. 10, ed. Philip Schaff and Henry Wace (Buffalo, NY: Christian Literature Publishing Co., 1896).

4 Irina Ratushinskaya, *Grey Is the Color of Hope*, trans. Alyona Kojevnikov (New York: Knopf, 1988), 75.

5 See James Bloodworth, *Hired: Six Months Undercover in Low-Wage Britain* (London: Atlantic Books, 2018).

6 David Graber, *Bullshit Jobs* (New York: Simon and Schuster, 2019).

7 Augustine, *Confessions*, 278 (13.9.10).

8 Augustine, *City of God*, trans. William Chase Greene (Cambridge, MA: Harvard University Press, 1969), vol. 6, 233 (19.24).

9 Marilynne Robinson, *Home* (New York: Macmillan, 2008), 104.

3. Aren't the Liberal Arts Elitist?

1 Nicholas B. Dirks, "The Liberal Arts and the University," *Center for Studies in Higher Education 7*, no. 15 (June 2015): 2.

2 James L. Hoerner, *An Historical Review of Liberal Education* (Coral Gables, FL: University of Miami, 1970), 2–4.

3 Hastings Rashdall, *The Universities of Europe in the Middle Ages* (Oxford University Press, 1997), 36.

4 This paragraph and next based on Thomas J. Denham, "A Brief History of the Major Components of the Medieval Setting" (doctoral thesis, Nova Southeastern University, 2002), 2–7.

5 Hoerner, 4–6.

6 Louis Paetow, "The Neglect of the Ancient Classics at the Early Medieval Universities," *Wisconsin Academy of Sciences, Arts and Letters* 16 (1908): 319.

7 Hoerner, 7.

8 "Boston Latin School," *Encyclopaedia Britannica*.

9 James Axtell, "The Death of the Liberal Arts College," *History of Education Quarterly* 11, no. 4 (1971): 339–40.

10 Hayley Glatter, "Throwback Thursday: Massachusetts Passes the Nation's First Compulsory Education Law," *Boston Magazine*, May 17, 2018.

11 Thomas D. Snyder, ed., *120 Years of American Education: A Statistical Portrait* (Washington, DC: National Center for Education Statistics, 1993), 55, 82.

12 Booker T. Washington, "The Fruits of Industrial Training," *The Atlantic*, October 1903.

13 Jennifer Frey, "Classics and Black History: Lessons from Dr. Anika Prather," The Thomas B. Fordham Institute, February 24, 2022. For more on these differing educational visions, see Angel Adams Parham's essay in chapter 5 of this book.

14 Dana Goldstein, *The Teacher Wars: A History of America's Most Embattled Profession* (New York: Anchor Books, 2015), 24.

15 NCES Fast Facts Tool, National Center for Education Statistics website.

16 "Great Books Reading List and Curriculum," St. John's College website.

17 Kara A. Godwin and Philip G. Altbach, "A Historical and Global Perspective on Liberal Arts Education," *International Journal of Chinese Education* 5, no. 1 (2016):15–18.

18 Horace Mann, "Report No. 12 of the Massachusetts School Board (1848)."

19 John Dewey, "My Pedagogic Creed," *School Journal* vol. 54 (January 1897), 77–80.

20 Patrick J. Deneen, "Strange Bedfellows: Allan Bloom and John Dewey against Liberal Education, Rightly Understood," *The Good Society* 17, no. 2 (2008): 49.

21 Eugene M. Lang, "Distinctively American: The Liberal Arts College," *Daedalus* 128, no. 1 (1999): 138.

22 Laura McInerney, "Snobbery about Vocational Education Is Denying Our Children Opportunities," *The Guardian*, January 21, 2014.

23 Adam Harris, "The Liberal Arts May Not Survive the 21st Century," *The Atlantic*, December 13, 2018.

24 Brandon McCoy, "Classical Education: An Attractive School Choice for Parents," Manhattan Institute, July 30, 2021.

25 Martha Nussbaum, "Education for Profit, Education for Freedom," *Liberal Education* (Summer 2009): 6; Godwin and Altbach, 5.

26 Martha Nussbaum, "Democracy, Education, and the Liberal Arts: Two Asian Models," *University of California at Davis Law Review* 44 (2011): 736–7.

27 Aristotle, *Metaphysics*, Trans. W. D. Ross (Arcadia E-Books, 2016), 1.2 (25).

28 Aristotle, *Metaphysics*, 1.2.

29 Robert M. Hutchins, *The Great Conversation: The Substance of a Liberal Education* (Encyclopaedia Britannica, 1952), 56.

30 Hutchins, 15–16.

31 Those interested can find out more at *catherineproject.org*.

4. Aren't the Liberal Arts Liberal?

1 Mitchell Langbert, Anthony J. Quain, and Daniel B. Klein, "Faculty Voter Registration in Economics, History, Law, Journalism, and Psychology," *Econ Journal Watch* 13, no. 3 (September 2016): 422–451. Note that this study looks at only a cross-section of humanities and social sciences disciplines and was conducted in 2016.

2 Flannery O'Connor, "Revelation" in *The Complete Stories of Flannery O'Connor* (New York: Farrar, Straus and Giroux, 1971), 488–509.

3 Jonathan Haidt, "Two Incompatible Sacred Values in American Universities," Hayek Lecture, Duke University (October 6, 2016).

4 "Report of the Committee on Freedom of Expression," University of Chicago, 2014. See also University of Chicago's Chancellor Emeritus Robert J. Zimmer, "Free Speech is the Basis of a True Education," *The Wall Street Journal*, August 26, 2016.

5 See Alasdair MacIntyre, *Three Rival Versions of Moral Enquiry* (Notre Dame, IN: University of Notre Dame Press, 1990), 225.

6 Augustine, *City of God*, trans. William Chase Greene (Cambridge, MA: Harvard University Press, 1969).

7 John M. Rist, *Augustine: Ancient Thought Baptized* (New York: Cambridge University Press, 1994).

8 See Friedrich Nietzsche's posthumously published essay, "On Truth and Lying in an Extra-Moral Sense," in *Friedrich Nietzsche on Rhetoric and Language*, ed. and trans. Sander L. Gilman, Carole Blair, and David J. Parent (New York: Oxford University Press, 1989).

9 MacIntyre, *Three Rival Versions*, 231.

5. Aren't the Liberal Arts Racist?

1 These are modern place names corresponding to the terms Herodotus used.

2 Herodotus, *The Histories*, trans. Robin Waterfield (Oxford: Oxford University Press, 2008), 96 (2.4).

3 See, for example, the treasure trove of artifacts and informative essays provided by the Metropolitan Museum of Art in its Egyptian Art Collections.

4 Homer, *The Odyssey, Books I–XII*, trans. Alexander Pope, ed. Maynard Mack (New Haven: Yale University Press, 1967), 30–31.

5 See Bonnie MacLachlan, "Feasting with Ethiopians: Life on the Fringe," *Quaderni Urbinati Di Cultura Classica* 40, no. 1 (1992): 15–33.

6 Herodotus, 178–179 (3.20).

7 Herodotus, 178–179 (3.23).

8 See Jim Al-Khalili, *The House of Wisdom: How Arabic Science Saved Ancient Knowledge and Gave Us the Renaissance*, (New York: Penguin Press, 2011); Jonathan Lyons, *The House of Wisdom: How the Arabs Transformed Western Civilization* (New York: Bloomsbury Publishing, 2011); Laurence Sigler, *Fibonacci's Liber Abaci: A Translation into Modern English of Leonardo Pisano's Book of Calculation* (New York: Springer, 2002).

9 This is by no means meant to imply that people of Africa and its diaspora were not already an active part of this conversation within their own communities, but now they began to address Western audiences.

10 See Hutchins, *The Great Conversation*; Mortimer Adler, *The Great Ideas: A Lexicon of Western Thought* (New York: Macmillan, 1992).

11 For a comprehensive anthology of texts on the Black intellectual tradition, see Henry Louis Gates and Jennifer Burton, eds. *Call and Response: Key Debates in African American Studies*. (New York: W. W. Norton, 2011).

12 Phillis Wheatley, "On Being Brought from Africa to America," in *The Collected Works of Phillis Wheatley*, ed. John Shields (New York: Oxford University Press, 1988), 18.

13 Phillis Wheatley, "Reverend and Honored Sir [To Samson Occom] (February 11, 1774)," in *The Collected Works of Phillis Wheatley*, 177.

14 For more on Douglass, see his *Narrative of the Life of Frederick Douglass, An American Slave* (New York: Dover Publications, 1995).

15 See especially *The Souls of Black Folk* (New York: Dover Publications, 1994) for this masterful weaving together of traditions. On the many classical allusions and influences on Du Bois's work, see David Withun, *Co-Workers in the Kingdom of Culture: Classics and Cosmopolitanism in the Thought of W. E. B. Du Bois* (New York: Oxford University Press, 2022).

16 Anna Julia Cooper, "On Education," in *The Voice of Anna Julia Cooper*, ed. Charles Lemert and Esme Bhan (New York: Rowman and Littlefield, 1998), 252.

17 See Marva Collins and Civia Tamarkin, *Marva Collins' Way* (New York: Penguin, 1990).

18 See Anika T. Prather and Angel Adams Parham, *The Black Intellectual Tradition: Reading Freedom in Classical Literature* (Camp Hill, PA: Classical Academic Press, 2022).

19 Oludamini Ogunnaike, "Of Cannons and Canons," *Renovatio*, December 11, 2018.

20 Alasdair MacInytre, "How to be a North American: A Lecture," Federation of State Humanities Councils (Washington, DC, 1988).

21 Recalling Stanley Hauerwas's dictum, "The primary task of Christian ethics involves an attempt to help us see. For we can only act within a world we can see and we can only see the world rightly by being trained

to see. We do not come to see just by looking, but by disciplined skills developed through initiation into a narrative." Stanley Hauerwas, "The Demands of a Truthful Story: Ethics and the Pastoral Task," *Chicago Studies* 21, no. 1 (1982): 65–66. Also see Stanley Hauerwas, "A Story-Formed Community: Reflections on *Watership Down*" in *The Hauerwas Reader*, ed. Michael Cartwright and John Berkman (Durham, NC: Duke University Press, 2001), 171–99.

22 Stanley Cavell, *Must We Mean What We Say? A Book of Essays* (Cambridge: Cambridge University Press, 2015), 1–43.

23 J. Peter Euben, "Imploding the Canon: The Reform of Education and the War Over Culture" in *Corrupting Youth Political Education, Democratic Culture, and Political Theory* (Princeton, NJ: Princeton University Press, 1997), 3–31.

24 See Rita Felski, *The Limits of Critique* (Chicago: University of Chicago Press, 2015).

25 Recently, see Keri Day, *Notes of a Native Daughter: Testifying in Theological Education* (Grand Rapids, MI: Eerdmans, 2021); Willie James Jennings, *After Whiteness: An Education in Belonging* (Grand Rapids, MI: Eerdmans, 2020); Roosevelt Montás, *Rescuing Socrates: How the Great Books Changed My Life and Why They Matter for a New Generation* (Princeton, NJ: Princeton University Press, 2021).

26 Stanley Cavell, *The Claim of Reason: Wittgenstein, Skepticism, Morality, and Tragedy* (New York: Oxford University Press, 1979).

27 For examples, see Saba Mahmood's account of mosque-based feminism, *Politics of Piety: The Islamic Revival and the Feminist Subject* (Princeton, NJ: Princeton University Press, 2005); Jonathan Lear's portrayal of Crow self-interpretation, *Radical Hope: Ethics in the Face of Cultural Devastation* (Cambridge, MA: Harvard University Press, 2006); and Cathleen Kaveny's rendition of the common-law tradition, "Law and Christian Ethics: Signposts for a Fruitful Conversation," *Journal of the Society of Christian Ethics* 35, no. 2 (2015): 3–32.

28 For Alasdair MacIntyre's formulations along these lines, see his *After Virtue: A Study in Moral Theory* (Notre Dame, IN: University of Notre Dame Press, 2016); *Whose Justice? Which Rationality?* (Notre Dame, IN: University of Notre Dame Press, 1988).

29 This proves no less true for communities that claim divine revelation for their canons. See Rowan Williams, *Arius: Heresy and Tradition* (London: Darton, Longman and Todd, 1987); Kevin Hector, *Theology without Metaphysics: God, Language, and the Spirit of Recognition* (Cambridge, UK ; Cambridge University Press, 2011); Natalie Carnes, *Image and Presence: A Christological Reflection on Iconoclasm and Iconophilia* (Stanford, CA: Stanford University Press, 2018).

30 See Stanley Cavell, *Pursuits of Happiness: The Hollywood Comedy of Remarriage* (Cambridge, MA: Harvard University Press, 1984).

31 Paul Reitter and Chad Wellmon, *Permanent Crisis: The Humanities in a Disenchanted Age* (Chicago: University of Chicago Press, 2021), 258–259.

6. Aren't the Liberal Arts Outdated?

1 Richard Darman, "Mid-Year Budget and Economic Review," speech, National Press Club, July 20, 1989.

2 L. Gregory Jones and Andrew P. Hogue, *Navigating the Future* (Nashville, TN: Abingdon, 2021), xviii–xix.

3 Jaroslav Pelikan, *The Vindication of Tradition* (New Haven, CT: Yale University Press, 1984), 65.

4 C. S. Lewis, *Surprised by Joy* (New York: Harcourt Brace & Company, 1955), 207–8.

5 Hans-Georg Gadamer, *Truth and Method*, trans. Joel Weinsheimer and Donald G. Marshall, 2nd rev. ed. (London: Sheed and Ward, 1999), 272–77. See also the work of people like Daniel Kahneman about the role that our intuitions and biases play in shaping most of our decisions. Kahneman, *Thinking, Fast and Slow* (New York: Farrar, Straus and Giroux, 2011).

6 Gadamer, 276–77.

7 Wendell Berry, *Standing by Words* (Washington, DC: Shoemaker & Hoard, 2005), 102.

8 Alan Jacobs, *Breaking Bread with the Dead* (New York: Penguin Press, 2020), 78.

9 MacIntyre, *Three Rival Versions*, 231.

10 George Santayana, *The Life of Reason* (Cambridge: MIT Press, 2011), 172.

11 Wilfred McKay, "The Claims of Memory," *First Things*, January 1, 2022.

12 Vincent Bacote, "In Search of a Truly Good News Faith," *Comment Magazine*, September 9, 2021. See also his book on Kuyper, *The Spirit in Public Theology* (Eugene, OR: Wipf and Stock, 2010).

13 Aubrey Streit Krug, "Grounded," *Center for Humans and Nature* (blog), September 8, 2017.

14 James D. Watson, *The Double Helix* (New York: Simon and Schuster, 1968).

7. Aren't the Liberal Arts Out of Touch?

1   2 Cor. 3:2–3 (NKJV).

2   Eph. 6:10–18 (NKJV).

3   Exod. 3:14 (NKJV).

4   Matt. 5:3–10 (NKJV).

5   Wheaton College, "The Mission of Wheaton College," accessed Dec. 30, 2022.

6   Calvin University, "Who We Are," accessed Dec. 30, 2022.

7   For a summary of the sorts of outcomes promised by liberal arts institutions and advocates through the centuries, see Richard Detweiler, *The Evidence Liberal Arts Needs: Lives of Consequence, Inquiry, and Accomplishment* (Cambridge, MA: MIT Press, 2021).

8   William Cronon, "Only Connect: The Goals of a Liberal Education," *The American Scholar* 67, no. 4 (1998): 73–80.

9   Jacques Ellul, "Needed: A New Karl Marx!" in *Sources and Trajectories: Eight Early Articles by Jacques Ellul that Set the Stage*, ed. Marva Dawn (Grand Rapids, MI: Eerdmans, 1997), 37.

10 By positioning inquiry as instrumental to greater relevance, I do not mean to suggest that inquiry *only* has instrumental value; inquiry also has intrinsic value. The balance of and relationship between inquiry and "relevance" in liberal arts education finds some parallels in debates about contemplation and action. For a helpful overview of and interesting perspective on those debates, see Jennifer Summit and Blakey Vermeule, *Action Versus Contemplation: Why an Ancient Debate Still Matters* (Chicago: University of Chicago Press, 2018).

11 See Erin Shaw, *Claim the Sky 2008*, erinshawart.com.

8. Aren't the Liberal Arts Unmarketable?

1 Jim Fong, "What the Numbers Tell Us: Re-Engineering the Liberal Arts Degree – A Baseline for the New Economy," *Unbound*, accessed October 13, 2022.

2 Vivek Wadhwa, "Why Liberal Arts and the Humanities Are as Important as Engineering," *The Washington Post*, June 12, 2018.

3 "Job Outlook 2019," National Association of College and Employers, November 2018.

4 Azami Zaharim et al., "Engineering Employability Skills Required by Employers in Asia," in *Proceedings of the 6th WSEAS International Conference on Engineering Education*, vol. 170 (2009).

5 Don Weinkauf, "Why Liberal Arts Is Essential to Engineering," University of St. Thomas website.

6 National Academy of Engineering, *The Engineer of 2020: Visions of Engineering in the New Century* (Washington, DC: National Academies Press, 2004).

7 David Deming, "In the Salary Race, Engineers Sprint but English Majors Endure," *The New York Times*, September 20, 2019.

8 Mark Edmundson, "The Ideal English Major," *The Chronicle of Higher Education*, July 29, 2013.

9 Anthony T. Kronman, *Education's End: Why Our Colleges and Universities Have Given Up on the Meaning of Life* (New Haven, CT: Yale University Press, 2007), 5.

10 Wes Jackson, *Becoming Native to This Place* (Berkeley, CA: Counterpoint, 1994), 3.

11 Jeffry C. Davis, "The Countercultural Quest of Christian Liberal Arts," in *Liberal Arts for the Christian Life*, eds. Jeffry C. Davis and Philip G. Ryken (Wheaton, IL: Crossway, 2012), 33.

12 Andrew Delbanco, *College: What It Was, Is, and Should Be* (Princeton, NJ: Princeton University Press, 2012), xv–xvi.

13 Detweiler, *The Evidence Liberal Arts Needs*.

14 Frank Bruni, "How to Get the Most Out of College," *The New York Times*, Aug. 17, 2018.

15 Karen An-hwei Lee, "Wheaton College as a Liberal Arts Institution," interviewed by Noah Toly, *The Liberating Arts*, Oct. 2, 2020.

16 Rosemary Barnes, "Job Ready University Degrees May Not Be the

Tertiary Education Solution We Are Hoping For," *ABC News*, Sept. 22, 2020.

17 "Dordt Will Begin Pro-Tech Programs," Dordt University, July 18, 2016.

18 Erik Hoekstra, "What the Liberal Arts Does (and Does Not) Have in Common with a Christian Education," interviewed by Rachel B. Griffis, *The Liberating Arts*, Nov. 10, 2020.

9. Aren't Liberal Arts Degrees a Luxury?

1 Albert J. Raboteau, *Slave Religion: The "Invisible Institution" in the Antebellum South* (Oxford: Oxford University Press, 2004).

2 Albert J. Raboteau, "Forgiveness and the African American Church Experience," *Faith Angle Forum*, November 2015.

3 Aristotle, *Nichomachean Ethics*, trans. Robert C. Bartlett and Susan D. Collins (Chicago: University of Chicago Press, 2012), Book 10.

4 See further my essay, "Befriending Books: On Reading and Thinking with Alan Jacobs and Zena Hitz," *Mere Orthodoxy*, November 23, 2020.

5 Denise Levertov, *The Collected Poems of Denise Levertov* (New York: New Directions, 2013) 861–862.

6 Gen. 11:1–9.

7 Patrick Kavanagh, "The Parish and the Universe," in *Poetry and Ireland Since 1800: A Source Book*, 204–206, edited by Mark Storey (London: Routledge, 1988), 204–206.

8 Bellow denied having said it, or at least in the way it was written. It was reported by James Atlas in his 1988 profile of Allan Bloom for the *New York Times Magazine*, "Chicago's Grumpy Guru."

9 Cited in Ta-Nehisi Coates, *Between the World and Me* (London: OneWorld Publishers, 2015), 56.

10 Dorothy L. Sayers, *Are Women Human?* (Grand Rapids, MI: Eerdmans, 1971).

11 See Book 1 of Boethius' *The Consolation of Philosophy*, trans. Victor Watts (London: Penguin Classics, 1999).

12 Possidius, *Vita*, 31.1–3; cited in Peter Brown, *Augustine of Hippo: A Biography* (Berkeley, CA: University of California Press, 2000), 436.

13 See G. K. Chesterton, *St. Thomas Aquinas: The Dumb Ox* (New York: Image Books, 1956).

14 See, for example, Robert Alter, *The Art of Biblical Poetry* (New York: Basic Books, 2011).

15 Rowan Williams, *Edge of Words: God and the Habits of Language* (New York: Bloomsbury, 2014), ix–xiii, 1–34.

16 Williams, 133.

17 Williams, 148.

18 Williams, 164.

19 See C. S. Lewis, *The Last Battle* (New York: Harper Trophy, 1956).

20 See Roger Scruton's remarks in *Culture Counts: Faith and Feeling in a World Besieged* (New York: Encounter Books, 2018), 62, 63–65.

21 Zena Hitz, *Lost in Thought: The Hidden Pleasures of an Intellectual Life* (Princeton, NJ: Princeton University Press, 2020), 142–43.

22 Josef Pieper, *Leisure: the Basis of Culture* (San Francisco: Ignatius Press, 2009), 46–47.

23 See Neil Prior, "Alabama church bombing victims honoured by Welsh window," *BBC News*, March 10, 2011. See further my essay, "Jewish Jesus, Black Christ," *Christian Century* 139:3 (February 9, 2022), 20–25.

24 William Shakespeare, *Julius Caesar* (Knoxville, TN: Wordsworth Editions, 1992), II.ii. 42–43 (60).

25 Aiyagari S. Mainali, et al., "Proceedings of the Second Curing Coma Campaign, NIH Symposium: Challenging the Future of Research for Coma and Disorders of Consciousness," *Neurocritical Care*, May 10, 2022.

26 L. S. Dugdale, *The Lost Art of Dying: Reviving Forgotten Wisdom* (New York: HarperOne, 2020), 212.

10. Aren't the Liberal Arts Just for Smart People?

1 Josiah Holbrook, "Associations of Adults for Mutual Education," *American Journal of Education* 1, no. 10 (October 1826): 594–97, quoted in Angela Ray, *Lyceum and Public Culture* (East Lansing, MI: Michigan State University Press, 2005), 194.

2 See Robert Putnam, *Bowling Alone* (New York: Simon & Schuster, 2000).

3 Aristotle, *Metaphysics*, 2 (980a21).

4 Anna Julia Cooper, *The Voice of Anna Julia Cooper*, 252.

5 Cooper, 251.

6 Cooper, 251.

7 J. Scott Lee, *Invention* (Sante Fe, NM: Respondeo Books, 2020), 22–23. Lee cites *Nicomachean Ethics*, VI.4 without a quotation.

8 See Fujimura's *Culture Care* (Westmont, IL: Intervarsity Press, 2017) or *Art and Faith* (New Haven, CT: Yale University Press, 2021); Crouch's *Culture Making* (Westmont, IL: Intervarsity Press, 2008); Sayers's *The Mind of the Maker* (New York: HarperCollins, 1987).

9 Ivan Illich, *Deschooling Society* (London: Calder & Boyars, 1971), 1.

10 Illich, 78.

11 O. Malamud, "Breadth Versus Depth: The Timing of Specialization in Higher Education," *Labour* 24, no. 4 (2010), 359–90.

12 David Epstein, *Range: Why Generalists Triumph in a Specialized World* (New York: Penguin Publishing Group, 2021).

13 Eberhard Arnold, "Reading Romans 13 under Fascism," *Plough Quarterly*, Spring 2020.

14 Friedrich Nietzsche, *Human, All Too Human*, trans. Marion Faber and Stephen Lehmann (Lincoln, NE: University of Nebraska Press, 1984), second supplement: "The Wanderer and His Shadow," aphorism 206.

15 Eberhard Arnold, *God's Revolution: Justice, Community, and the Coming Kingdom*, 3rd ed. (Walden, NY: Plough Publishing House, 2021), 122.

Bibliography

Adler, Mortimer. *The Great Ideas: A Lexicon of Western Thought.* New York: Macmillan, 1992.

Al-Khalili, Jim. *The House of Wisdom: How Arabic Science Saved Ancient Knowledge and Gave Us the Renaissance.* New York: Penguin Press, 2011.

Alter, Robert. *The Art of Biblical Poetry.* New York: Basic Books, 2011.

Ambrose. *Concerning Virginity.* Translated by H. de Romestin, E. de Romestin, and H. T. F. Duckworth. In *Nicene and Post-Nicene Fathers, Second Series*, Vol. 10. Edited by Philip Schaff and Henry Wace. Buffalo, NY: Christian Literature Publishing Co., 1896.

Aristotle. *Metaphysics.* Translated by W. D. Ross. Arcadia E-Books, 2016.

———. *Nichomachean Ethics.* Translated by Robert C. Bartlett and Susan D. Collins. Chicago: University of Chicago Press, 2012.

Arnold, Eberhard. *God's Revolution: Justice, Community, and the Coming Kingdom*, 3rd ed. Walden, NY: Plough Publishing House, 2021.

———. "Reading Romans 13 under Fascism." *Plough Quarterly*, Spring 2020.

Augustine. *Confessions.* Translated by Henry Chadwick. Oxford: Oxford University Press, 2009.

———. *City of God.* Translated by William Chase Greene. Cambridge, MA: Harvard University Press, 1969.

Axtell, James. "The Death of the Liberal Arts College." *History of Education Quarterly* 11, no. 4 (1971): 339–52.

Bacote, Vincent. "In Search of a Truly Good News Faith." *Comment Magazine.* September 9, 2021.

———. *The Spirit in Public Theology.* Eugene, OR: Wipf and Stock, 2010.

Barnes, Rosemary. "Job Ready University Degrees May Not Be the Tertiary Education Solution We Are Hoping For." *ABC News.* Sept. 22, 2020.

Berry, Wendell. *Standing by Words.* Washington, D.C.: Shoemaker & Hoard, 2005.

Bilbro, Jeffrey. "Going Dark." *Breaking Ground*, September 29, 2020.

Bloodworth, James. *Hired: Six Months Undercover in Low-Wage Britain.* London: Atlantic Books, 2018.

Boethius. *The Consolation of Philosophy*. Translated by Victor Watts. London: Penguin Classics, 1999.

Brown, Peter. *Augustine of Hippo: A Biography*. Berkeley: University of California Press, 2000.

Bruni, Frank. "How to Get the Most Out of College." *The New York Times*. August 17, 2018.

Carnes, Natalie. *Image and Presence: A Christological Reflection on Iconoclasm and Iconophilia*. Stanford, CA: Stanford University Press, 2018.

Cavell, Stanley. *The Claim of Reason: Wittgenstein, Skepticism, Morality, and Tragedy*. New York: Oxford University Press, 1979.

———. *Must We Mean What We Say? A Book of Essays*. Cambridge: Cambridge University Press, 2015.

———. *Pursuits of Happiness: The Hollywood Comedy of Remarriage*. Cambridge, MA: Harvard University Press, 1984.

Chesterton, G. K. *St. Thomas Aquinas: The Dumb Ox*. New York: Image Books, 1956.

Coates, Ta-Nehisi. *Between the World and Me*. London: OneWorld Publishers, 2015.

Coffey, Clare, Rob Sentz and Yustina Saleh. "Degrees at Work: Examining the Serendipitous Outcomes of Diverse Degrees." EMSI Profile Analytics. August 2019.

Collins, Marva, and Civia Tamarkin. *Marva Collins' Way*. New York: Penguin, 1990.

Cooper, Anna Julia. *The Voice of Anna Julia Cooper*. Edited by Charles Lemert and Esme Bhan. Lanham, MD: Rowman & Littlefield Publishers, 1998.

Cronon, William. "Only Connect: The Goals of a Liberal Education." *The American Scholar* 67, no. 4 (1998): 73–80.

Crouch, Andy. *Culture Making*. Westmont, IL: Intervarsity Press, 2008.

Darman, Richard. "Mid-Year Budget and Economic Review." Speech. National Press Club, July 20, 1989.

Davis, Jeffrey C. "The Countercultural Quest of Christian Liberal Arts." In *Liberal Arts for the Christian Life*, 31–45. Edited by Jeffrey C. Davis and Philip G. Ryken. Wheaton, IL: Crossway, 2012.

Day, Keri. *Notes of a Native Daughter: Testifying in Theological Education*. Grand Rapids, MI: Eerdmans, 2021.

Delbanco, Andrew. *College: What It Was, Is, and Should Be.* Princeton: Princeton University Press, 2012.

Deming, David. "In the Salary Race, Engineers Sprint but English Majors Endure." *The New York Times.* September 20, 2019.

Deneen, Patrick J. "Strange Bedfellows: Allan Bloom and John Dewey against Liberal Education, Rightly Understood." *The Good Society* 17, no. 2 (2008): 49–55.

Denhem, Thomas J. "A Brief History of the Major Components of the Medieval Setting." Doctoral thesis, Nova Southeastern University, 2002.

Detweiler, Richard A. *The Evidence Liberal Arts Needs: Lives of Consequence, Inquiry, and Accomplishment.* Cambridge: The MIT Press, 2021.

Dewey, John. "My Pedagogic Creed," *School Journal* vol. 54 (January 1897), 77–80.

Dirks, Nicholas B. "The Liberal Arts and the University." *Center for Studies in Higher Education* 7, no. 15 (June 2015).

Du Bois, W. E. B. *The Souls of Black Folk.* New York: Dover Publications, 1994.

Dugdale, L. S. *The Lost Art of Dying: Reviving Forgotten Wisdom.* New York: HarperOne, 2020.

Edmundson, Mark. "The Ideal English Major." *The Chronicle of Higher Education.* July 29, 2013.

Epstein, David. Range: *Why Generalists Triumph in a Specialized World.* New York: Penguin Publishing Group, 2021.

Ellul, Jacques. "Needed: A New Karl Marx!" In *Sources and Trajectories: Eight Early Articles by Jacques Ellul that Set the Stage.* Edited by Marva Dawn. Grand Rapids: Eerdmans, 1997.

Euben, J. Peter. "Imploding the Canon: The Reform of Education and the War Over Culture." In *Corrupting Youth Political Education, Democratic Culture, and Political Theory*, 3–31. Princeton, NJ: Princeton University Press, 1997.

Felski, Rita. *The Limits of Critique.* Chicago: University of Chicago Press, 2015.

Fong, Jim. "What the Numbers Tell Us: Re-Engineering the Liberal Arts Degree – A Baseline for the New Economy." *Unbound.* Accessed October 13, 2022.

Frey, Jennifer. "Classics and Black History: Lessons from Dr. Anika Prather," The Thomas B. Fordham Institute, February 24, 2022.

Fujimura, Makoto. *Art and Faith*. New Haven, CT: Yale University Press, 2021.

———. *Culture Care*. Westmont, IL: Intervarsity Press, 2017.

Gadamer, Hans Georg. *Truth and Method*. Translated by Joel Weinsheimer and Donald G. Marshall. London: Sheed and Ward, 1999.

Gates, Henry Louis, and Jennifer Burton, eds. *Call and Response: Key Debates in African American Studies*. New York: W.W. Norton, 2011.

Glatter, Hayley. "Throwback Thursday: Massachusetts Passes the Nation's First Compulsory Education Law." *Boston Magazine*. May 17, 2018.

Godwin, Kara A., and Phillip Altbach. "A Historical and Global Perspective on Liberal Arts Education," *International Journal of Chinese Education* 5, no. 1 (2016).

Goldstein, Dana. *The Teacher Wars: A History of America's Most Embattled Profession*. New York: Anchor Books, 2015.

Graber, David. *Bullshit Jobs*. New York: Simon and Schuster, 2019.

"Great Books Reading List and Curriculum." St. John's College. Accessed June 6, 2022.

Haidt, Jonathan. "Two incompatible sacred values in American universities." Hayek Lecture, Duke University. October 6, 2016.

Harris, Adam. "The Liberal Arts May Not Survive the 21st Century." *The Atlantic*. December 13, 2018.

Hauerwas, Stanley. "A Story-Formed Community: Reflections on Watership Down." In *The Hauerwas Reader*, 171–99. Edited by Michael Cartwright and John Berkman. Durham, NC: Duke University Press, 2001.

———. "The Demands of a Truthful Story: Ethics and the Pastoral Task." *Chicago Studies* 21, no. 1 (1982): 59–71.

Hector, Kevin. *Theology without Metaphysics: God, Language, and the Spirit of Recognition*. Cambridge, UK: Cambridge University Press, 2011.

Herodotus. *The Histories*. Translated by Robin Watterfield. Oxford: Oxford University Press, 2008.

Heschel, Abraham Joshua. *The Sabbath*. New York: Farrar, Straus and Giroux, 2005 [1951].

Hitz, Zena. *Lost in Thought: The Hidden Pleasures of an Intellectual Life.* Princeton: Princeton University Press, 2020.

Hoekstra, Erik. "What the Liberal Arts Does (and Does Not) Have in Common with a Christian Education." Interviewed by Rachel B. Griffis. *The Liberating Arts* (blog). November 10, 2020.

Hoener, James L. *An Historical Review of Liberal Education.* Coral Gables, FL: University of Miami, 1970.

Homer. *The Odyssey, Books I-XII.* Translated by Alexander Pope. Edited by Maynard Mack. New Haven: Yale University Press, 1967.

Hutchins, Robert M. *The Great Conversation: The Substance of a Liberal Education.* Encyclopaedia Britannica, 1952.

Illich, Ivan. *Deschooling Society.* London: Calder & Boyars, 1971.

Jackson, Wes. *Becoming Native to This Place.* Berkeley: Counterpoint, 1994.

Jacobs, Alan. *Breaking Bread with the Dead.* New York: Penguin Press, 2020.

Jennings, Willie James. *After Whiteness: An Education in Belonging.* Grand Rapids, MI: Eerdmans, 2020.

"Job Outlook 2019." National Association of College and Employers. November 2018.

Jones, L. Gregory, and Andrew P. Hogue. *Navigating the Future.* Nashville: Abingdon, 2021.

Kahneman, Daniel. *Thinking, Fast and Slow.* New York: Farrar, Straus and Giroux, 2011.

Kavanagh, Patrick. "The Parish and the Universe." In *Poetry and Ireland Since 1800: A Source Book*, 204–206. Edited by Mark Storey. London: Routledge, 1988.

Kaveny, Cathleen. "Law and Christian Ethics: Signposts for a Fruitful Conversation." In *Journal of the Society of Christian Ethics* 35, no. 2 (2015): 3–32.

Kronman, Anthony T. *Education's End: Why Our Colleges and Universities Have Given Up on the Meaning of Life.* New Haven: Yale University Press, 2007.

Krug, Aubrey Streit. "Grounded," *Center for Humans and Nature* (blog), September 8, 2017.

Lang, Eugene M. "Distinctively American: The Liberal Arts College." *Daedalus* 128, no. 1 (1999): 133–150.

Langbert, Mitchell, Anthony J. Quain, and Daniel B. Klein. "Faculty Voter Registration in Economics, History, Law, Journalism, and Psychology." *Econ Journal Watch* 13, no. 3 (September 2016): 422–451.

Lear, Jonathan. *Radical Hope: Ethics in the Face of Cultural Devastation.* Cambridge, MA: Harvard University Press, 2006.

Lee, J. Scott. *Invention.* Sante Fe, NM: Respondeo Books, 2020.

Lee, Karen An-hwei. "Wheaton College as a Liberal Arts Institution." Interviewed by Noah Toly. *The Liberating Arts* (blog). October 2, 2020.

Lewis, C. S. *The Last Battle.* New York: HarperTrophy, 1956.

———. *Surprised by Joy.* New York: Harcourt Brace, 1955.

Levertov, Denise. *The Collected Poems of Denise Levertov.* New York: New Directions, 2013.

Lyons, Jonathan. *The House of Wisdom: How the Arabs Transformed Western Civilization.* New York: Bloomsbury Publishing, 2011.

MacInytre, Alasdair. *After Virtue: A Study in Moral Theory.* Notre Dame, IN: University of Notre Dame Press, 2016.

———. "How to be a North American." Lecture at the Federation of State Humanities Councils, Washington, DC, 1988.

———. *Three Rival Versions of Moral Enquiry.* Notre Dame, IN: University of Notre Dame Press, 1991.

———. *Whose Justice? Which Rationality?* Notre Dame, IN: University of Notre Dame Press, 1988.

MacLachlan, Bonnie. "Feasting with Ethiopians: Life on the Fringe." *Quaderni Urbinati Di ultura Classica* 40, no. 1 (1992): 15–33.

Mahmood, Saba. *Politics of Piety: The Islamic Revival and the Feminist Subject.* Princeton, NJ: Princeton University Press, 2005.

Mainali, Aiyagari S., et al. "Proceedings of the Second Curing Coma Campaign, NIH Symposium: Challenging the Future of Research for Coma and Disorders of Consciousness." *Neurocritical Care.* May 10, 2022.

Malamud, O. "Breadth Versus Depth: The Timing of Specialization in Higher Education." *Labour* 24, no. 4 (2010): 359–90.

Mann, Horace. "Report No. 12 of the Massachusetts School Board (1848)."

McCoy, Brandon. "Classical Education: An Attractive School Choice for Parents," Manhattan Institute. July 30, 2021.

McKay, Wilfred. "The Claims of Memory." *First Things.* January 1, 2022.

McInerney, Laura. "Snobbery about Vocational Education Is Denying Our Children Opportunities." *The Guardian.* January 21, 2014.

Montás, Roosevelt. *Rescuing Socrates: How the Great Books Changed My Life and Why They Matter for a New Generation.* Princeton, NJ: Princeton University Press, 2021.

National Academy of Engineering. *The Engineer of 2020: Visions of Engineering in the New Century.* Washington, DC: National Academies Press, 2004.

NCES Fast Facts Tool. National Center for Education Statistics website.

Nietzsche, Friedrich. *Human, All Too Human.* Translated by Marion Faber and Stephen Lehmann. Lincoln: University of Nebraska Press, 1984.

———. "On Truth and Lying in an Extra-Moral Sense." In *Friedrich Nietzsche on Rhetoric and Language*, edited and translated by Sander L. Gilman, Carole Blair, and David J. Parent. New York: Oxford University Press, 1989.

Nussbaum, Martha. "Democracy, Education, and the Liberal Arts: Two Asian Models." *University of California at Davis Law Review* 44 (2011): 736–7.

———. "Education for Profit, Education for Freedom," *Liberal Education* (Summer 2009): 6.

O'Connor, Flannery. "Revelation." In *The Complete Stories of Flannery O'Connor*, 488–509. New York: Farrar, Straus and Giroux, 1971.

Ogunnaike, Oludamini. "Of Cannons and Canons." *Renovatio.* December 11, 2018.

Paetow, Louis. "The Neglect of the Ancient Classics at the Early Medieval Universities." Wisconsin Academy of Sciences, Arts and Letters 16 (1908): 311–19.

Pieper, Josef. *Leisure: The Basis of Culture.* San Francisco: Ignatius Press, 2009.

Pelikan, Jaroslav. *The Vindication of Tradition.* New Haven: Yale University Press, 1984.

Prather, Anika T., and Angel Adams Parham. *The Black Intellectual Tradition: Reading Freedom in Classical Literature.* Camp Hill, PA: Classical Academic Press, 2022.

Prior, Neil. "Alabama church bombing victims honoured by Welsh window." BBC News. March 10, 2011.

Putnam, Robert. *Bowling Alone*. New York: Simon & Schuster, 2000.

Raboteau, Albert J. "Forgiveness and the African American Church Experience," *Faith Angle Forum*, November 2015.

———. *Slave Religion: The "Invisible Institution" in the Antebellum South*. Oxford: Oxford University Press, 2004.

Rashdall, Hastings. *The Universities of Europe in the Middle Ages*. Oxford University Press, 1997.

Ratushinskaya, Irina. *Grey Is the Color of Hope*. Translated by Alyona Kojevnikov. New York: Knopf, 1988.

Ray, Angela. *Lyceum and Public Culture*. East Lansing, MI: Michigan State University Press, 2005.

Reitter, Paul, and Chad Wellmon. *Permanent Crisis: The Humanities in a Disenchanted Age*. Chicago: University of Chicago Press, 2021.

"Report of the Committee on Freedom of Expression." University of Chicago. 2014.

Rist, John M. *Augustine: Ancient Thought Baptized*. New York: Cambridge University Press, 1994.

Robinson, Marilynne. *Home*. New York: Macmillan, 2008.

Santayana, George. *The Life of Reason*. Cambridge: MIT Press, 2011.

Sayers, Dorothy L. *Are Women Human?* (Grand Rapids, MI: Eerdmans, 1971).

———. *The Mind of the Maker*. New York: HarperCollins, 1987.

Schwehn, Mark. *Exiles from Eden: Religion and the Academic Vocation in America*. Oxford: Oxford University Press, 1993.

Scruton, Roger. *Culture Counts: Faith and Feeling in a World Besieged*. New York: Encounter Books, 2018.

Shakespeare, William. *Julius Caesar*. Knoxville, TN: Wordsworth Editions, 1992.

Shaw, Erin. "Claim the Sky 2008." erinshawart.com.

Sigler, Laurence. *Fibonacci's Liber Abaci: A Translation into Modern English of Leonardo Pisano's Book of Calculation*. New York: Springer, 2002.

Snyder, Thomas D., ed. "120 Years of American Education: A Statistical Portrait." National Center for Education Statistics, 1993.

Summit, Jennifer, and Blakey Vermeule. *Action Versus Contemplation: Why an Ancient Debate Still Matters*. Chicago: University of Chicago Press, 2018.

Wadha, Vivek. "Why Liberal Arts and the Humanities Are as Important as Engineering," *The Washington Post*, June 12, 2018.

Washington, Booker T. "The Fruits of Industrial Training." *The Atlantic*. July 12, 2018.

Watson, James D. *The Double Helix*. New York: Simon and Schuster, 1968.

Weinkauf, Don. "Why Liberal Arts Is Essential to Engineering." University of St. Thomas website.

Wheatley, Phillis. *The Collected Works of Phillis Wheatley*. Edited by John Shields. New York: Oxford University Press. 1988.

Williams, Rowan. *Arius: Heresy and Tradition*. London: Darton, Longman and Todd, 1987.

———. *Edge of Words: God and the Habits of Language*. New York: Bloomsbury, 2014.

Withun, David. *Co-Workers in the Kingdom of Culture: Classics and Cosmopolitanism in the Thought of W. E. B. Du Bois*. New York: Oxford University Press, 2022.

Zaharim, Azami, et al. "Engineering Employability Skills Required by Employers in Asia." In *Proceedings of the 6th WSEAS International Conference on Engineering Education*, vol. 170 (2009).

Zimmer, Robert J. "Free Speech is the Basis of a True Education," *The Wall Street Journal*, August 26, 2016.